To my dear friend Virginia
God's blessings!
Randy Kennedy
Ecclesiastes 12:13

KINGDOM
WARRIORS

KINGDOM WARRIORS

*Victorious Through Radical
Devotion to God*

RANDY KENNEDY

XULON PRESS

Xulon Press
2301 Lucien Way #415
Maitland, FL 32751
407.339.4217
www.xulonpress.com

Unless otherwise indicated, Scripture quotations taken from the Holy Bible, New International Version (NIV). Copyright © 1973, 1978, 1984, 2011 by Biblica, Inc.™. Used by permission. All rights reserved.)

Paperback ISBN-13: 978-1-6322-1156-9

Ebook ISBN-13: 978-1-6322-1157-6

Randy is available to speak at your church, retreat, or other event

randykennedykingdombooks.com

Also available in audio or e-book

"...that in all things he might have the pre-eminence."
Colossians 1:18 (KJV)

TABLE OF CONTENTS

INTRODUCTION

I am now just over a half-century old (ouch!) and the world has changed dramatically during my lifetime. When I was a child in the 1960's, the vast majority of people went to church on Sunday mornings and Christianity was undeniably the prominent spiritual belief in the United States. To most Americans, the now headline-dominating religion of Islam was merely a curiosity largely centered in the Middle East.

I find it interesting when I think back to the sitcom, *I Dream of Jeannie*. Unless you have been...uh...trapped in a bottle since the 60's, I'm sure you know about the show. Jeannie had been imprisoned in her bottle for many years until an astronaut, Major Tony Nelson, found it and pulled the cap off setting Jeannie free.

The reason I bring this up is because the show captured the essence of what we in the United States thought of the Middle East at that time. Jeannie's fictional relatives from Baghdad would occasionally make appearances on the show. They would be comically dressed in clothes more likely worn during a previous century or two, and their humorless demeanor was, oddly enough, quite humorous. But I remember thinking *that* was the way it really was in modern day Iraq. It was a place that might as well have been a million miles away. And the dominant religion of that region, Islam, seemed to be just as distant.

But over the last 50 years my perception, and reality, have certainly undergone a major transformation. Baghdad is no longer an obscure place that time has left behind. Instead, it is a modern city where people may have a darker complexion than most Americans, but they often look a lot like us in their Western-influenced attire. And it is a place of deep pain for many who have lost loved ones in a war against a terrible evil called radical Islam. At its core, this evil is orchestrated in the pits of hell itself.

Despite the violent "holy war" they wage in Iraq and much of the Middle East, the radical Muslims have been unable to damage the reputation of Islam. It is a religion that is continuing to make advances around the world, as well as here in the United States, because of a carefully waged public relations campaign. I discussed this in the first book in this series, *Kingdom Invaders: Postmodern Threats to Biblical Christianity*.[1]

Most of the world, including your average Muslim American, is quite naive to the actual teachings of the Qur'an, the Islamic "holy book." They would point to several surahs, or chapters, that encourage a peaceful co-existence with people of other faiths. But the violent chapters which call for holy war, or jihad, were written later. In Islamic doctrine these abrogate, or replace, the peaceful chapters. So the so-called "extremists" are actually more tuned in to what Mohammed, the founder of Islam, had in mind some 15 centuries ago. But the depiction of Islam as a "peaceful" religion is only one of the reasons it has begun to make great advances in the United States.

The late Nabeel Qureshi, author of the book *Seeking Allah, Finding Jesus*[2] was a former Muslim who became a devout believer in Jesus Christ. At a Q and A on March 22nd, 2015 at Christ Community Chapel in Hudson, Ohio, he was asked by a member of the audience why he thought Muslims were more passionate than Christians in the practice of their faith. (This was about 2 1/2 years prior to his untimely death due to cancer.)

Qureshi said he believed the perceived passion that is found in Islam comes from the fact that Muslims don't understand the concept of biblical grace, so they have no assurance of salvation. Therefore, they are continually working to gain favor with their god, Allah.

Conversely, Qureshi said he believed the typical Christian's embrace of biblical grace has actually been taken way too far. Instead of letting God's unmerited favor drive us lovingly toward impassioned service for the cause of Christ, he said we have taken advantage of that grace to merely say, "I'm going to heaven, so I'm fine." Qureshi said that has lulled us into a sense of complacency, making us into "lukewarm" Christians.

I agree wholeheartedly with Qureshi's assessment. These two factors related to grace, which have prompted diametrically opposed responses, have been significant factors in the alarming advance of Islam in our traditionally Christian-dominant nation. And I will make the contention in this book that the growth of Islam, as well as many other false spiritual beliefs, is one of the residual effects of a Christian Church that has largely lost its "saltiness" as Jesus discussed in Matthew 5:13.

Unlike *Kingdom Invaders*, which was a message addressed to skeptics as well as believers in Jesus, *Kingdom Warriors* is written specifically to Christians. It is a call for individual consecration to God as a way of building His Kingdom from within; a return to a powerful Church that is truly salt and light. Today, we are no longer "flavoring" the culture around us, and that is leaving a spiritual void that is happily being filled by other false religions and beliefs.

If you need more evidence of the diminished influence of Christianity in the U.S. you need not look further than the redefinition of marriage. Legally, it no longer conforms to God's design of one man with one woman for life (Genesis 2:22-24). Instead, marriage is now allowed in the case of any two people who "love" each other. It remains to be seen if that definition will continue changing to include more than two people, or something even more perverse.

There is also an ever-growing belief in our formerly Christian-dominant culture that Jesus no longer matters when it comes to salvation. It is thought that there are so many good people in other religions — such as Islam, Hinduism, Buddhism, Mormonism, Jehovah's Witnesses, etc. — that perhaps Christians are wrong. This comes despite the clear directives in the Bible telling us that making Jesus our Savior and Lord is the only way that we can live eternally with God (John 10:9, John 10:28, John 14:6, John 17:2-3, Romans 5:9, 2 Corinthians 5:21, 1 John 5:11-12, etc.).

I truly believe the main reason that biblical precepts are no longer respected in our culture, and our God no longer honored, is that the average believer in Jesus looks almost exactly like everybody else. The world has created its own version of what is moral. Sadly, the Church too often today is agreeing with this version, whether it is biblical or not.

The Greek word "ekklesia," often translated in the New Testament as "the church," means "called out ones." In other words, by definition, we as believers are supposed to be set apart and different — *in* the world but not *of* it (1 John 2:15). Instead, the typical person who claims to be a Christian in the U.S. is very comfortable dwelling in these worldly surroundings and participating in the questionable — if not downright sinful — attitudes, actions, and activities of everybody else. And when they do, they are often embraced by the world as being loving, accepting, and tolerant — but to what eternal cost?

The percentage of Americans who call themselves born-again Christians drops every year. Church attendance is continuing a downward trend. And those who do go to church often attend large, feel-good fellowships which teach a kinder, gentler gospel that ignores the requirement for sacrificial lives of service to God. Rather than coldly looking at these developments as mere disappointments, we need to grasp the reality that these are precious souls who may be facing an eternity in the torment of hell.

Many years ago our small-town church hosted a picnic and softball game following a Sunday morning service. One lady in attendance that day said to me that if the church did more things like this then the membership would certainly grow. That may very well have been true. But this lady was a tiny representation of a much bigger problem in many of today's churches. The only times she ever showed up were when our church was doing the "fun stuff." She had no intention of seeking spiritual maturity.

Should it really be our goal to bring in more people if they are only there to enjoy the "country club" atmosphere of our churches? Or are we going to make sure that the presentation of biblical truth is of the utmost importance?

I realize that it is regularly pastors of the mega-churches who get the book deals and invites to radio, TV, and even worldwide conferences. But what kind of Christian culture is being created if the Gospel message is not front and center and shared in full counsel? Are the people who come to these churches merely being superficially entertained by special events and activities? Or are they regularly being trained to become mature, sacrificial servants of the Lord?

These massive churches and their pastors would give you the impression that Christianity is alive and well, and growing healthy and strong in America. But it should only take a quick glance at the moral free fall of our nation, and its sprint away from true biblical Christianity, to realize that the way we have been doing things as believers in recent years simply isn't working.

Those who own a service business are generally mindful of the importance of promoting their high-quality product in virtually every aspect of their lives. If what they say and do does not match the value of the product they are trying to sell, then the consumer may reject it — no matter how great the product might be.

Similarly, as Christians we need to promote the high-quality "product" we are trying to sell in every aspect of our lives. Of course, that would be Jesus. If what we say and do does not match the tremendous value of the Gospel message, then the "consumer" may reject our Lord — even though He is the greatest and most important "product" of all time. With that in mind, it is my prayer that we begin to sense the critical importance of living as consecrated vessels that point to the true Gospel and the salvation available through Jesus.

You will soon see that I do something in this book that is seldom, if ever, done. I will be quite specific when it comes to our behaviors as Christians. I understand why no one wants to attempt such a thing; there is great disagreement among sincere believers on many of the issues I'll be discussing.

But there was a time in my life when I was trying to reconcile what I believed to be righteous Christ-like behavior, with what I perceived to be ungodly behavior in the lives of many others who called themselves Christians. I could find no definitive source of help to ease my confusion.

You could say the Bible should have been that source, but these other people with very different lifestyles and convictions said they based their beliefs on the Scriptures as well. So further direction seemed necessary. With that as my catalyst, I began a process of studying the Bible, researching historical and statistical perspectives, and spending daily time in prayer asking God to reveal His heart to me about the various issues I will be discussing.

Now, where two or three are gathered together reading this book they may end up laughing at me. I know this because I have occasionally heard Christians making fun of some of my sincerely held beliefs about these topics when they didn't know

I disagreed with them. As you read you may be tempted to do the same, thinking of me as some sort of out-of-touch fundamentalist. But I would humbly ask that you please seriously consider the arguments I am making and pray that the Holy Spirit will speak God's truth to you.

This book is all about raising the bar on how we live our lives as Christians. Many of the issues I discuss, which were at one time taken seriously for their potential to cause spiritual harm, are now often met with a belittling roll of the eyes if I bring them up as areas of genuine concern. This change has come about in just a generation or two. And it has become apparent to me that as the morality and standards of the culture have quickly deteriorated in recent years, so too have the morality and standards diminished among those who would call themselves Christians. It's true that the Christian standards remain higher, but sadly, not by much.

Through these pages I'll be making an attempt to reconcile our past as Christians with the present, with an eye on the future. As I've already mentioned, the status quo today is clearly not working. And I truly believe that if each one of us individually commits to a greater personal consecration to God, we can play a significant role in turning the cultural tide toward righteousness and morality — and ultimately, toward belief in Jesus — one life at a time. It is my prayer that as you read, you will notice a growing desire in your heart to further commit yourself to the Lord — becoming a spiritual warrior that can be used by God to win ongoing victories for His Kingdom!

[Handwritten margin note, right side:] How we live is critical. On fire, who he is & our identity in Him - speaking from faith & love focused on

[Handwritten note, bottom:] Why is that the goal?! Like yes, wanting culture to turn & see Him & believe is the goal but - this sentence sounds so behavored. Like if we just pull our selves up by our bootstraps & commit we will do this thing!" Or how about I fall so in love w/ Him & he's my focus that I can't help but look like love & shine. Same end goal maybe, diff. heart.

1–LEGALISM AND LIBERTY

Man-made rules should not be used to somehow establish our spirituality, gain favor with God, or be "good enough" for salvation. Rather, they should be used prudently to create boundaries or safeguards against falling into sin.

O ur neighbors had a dog named Riley. One time when they were planning on going away for a week to visit relatives, they asked me if I could take care of her. They had a kennel for Riley, about 12 feet long by 6 feet wide, so they said it wouldn't be too hard to watch her; just give her some fresh water and a scoop of food each day. Since I took a walk of about a mile each day on our country road, I asked them if it would be OK if I brought Riley with me. They said that would be fine and that she was always good about "kenneling up" so it wouldn't be hard to get her back in when I was done.

As I would come to get Riley each day, she would start barking excitedly when she saw me walking up the driveway. She was from a breed that absolutely loves to run, so when I would open the kennel gate she would fly out of there like an overfilled balloon with a sudden release of air. And for about the next half-hour I had so much fun watching Riley run free with no particular destination in mind. Back and forth on the road, and to and fro in the adjacent fields, she would stop only momentarily when her sensitive nose picked up a scent worth investigating.

1

Through it all, I noticed Riley would take an occasional glance back at me just to make sure I wasn't too far away. And the only time I would have to rein her in was when an element of danger presented itself, like when a car was approaching or she was nearing the home of a large dog.

After several days of this, it occurred to me that my walks with Riley were providing some wonderful parallels for what I'm going to be discussing in the next two chapters. *Legalism* was being represented by Riley in the kennel. When I opened the gate and she ran free, that was analogous of *liberty* in Christ. And when I called Riley to my side in the midst of danger, that was representative of a constraint of freedom for the sake of *love*.

THE KENNEL OF LEGALISM

In my first book, *Kingdom Invaders*, I gave several examples of people who were proponents of what I called "Grace Gone Wild." These were people who in my belief overemphasized the grace of God over His other attributes, such as justice and hatred of sin. I found it to be interesting that these people often had one thing in common — they experienced a great deal of legalism in their homes when they were growing up. They were told to toe the line of Christian belief or face serious consequences. This ranged from the clearly sinful behaviors mentioned in the Bible to those that may have been added at the discretion of man. I'd like to tell you two such stories of men who grew up in the "kennel" of legalism.

The first man, I'll call Edward, gave me tremendous insight into why he had an "almost anything goes" mentality toward his Christian faith. He grew up in a home where the most important thing you did to please God was keep the rules — not just Bible-based commandments, but also man-made dictates. If you didn't drink, dance, smoke, chew, (or go with those who do) then you were pleasing God.

2

But the problem was that the same parents who adamantly enforced these rules were also often times overbearing, critical, and harsh toward Edward. The fruit of the Spirit – love, joy, peace, patience, kindness, goodness, gentleness, etc. – was too often absent when Edward's parents would interact with him. So in his mind, if being a Christian kept you from doing certain things that seemed enjoyable or fun, yet allowed you to cause pain to those you are supposed to love, then why would you want to be a part of that?

The other man grew up in the same holiness background that I had come from. I'll call him Andrew. The founding fathers of our denomination came up with a list of rules prohibiting such things as drinking, smoking, gambling, and dancing. Even though our spiritual backgrounds were similar, somewhere along the line Andrew came to believe that if he did these or any number of other things on a list of "don'ts" that he would go to hell. I was stunned to hear this.

As this book continues you will see that I don't endorse any of these activities, but I certainly don't believe that in and of themselves they will condemn a person to hell. Did Andrew receive false teaching from a Sunday school teacher or some other church leader? Was it simply a misconception? Did the powers of darkness create confusion in Andrew's mind, veiling him from understanding the truth? Or was it a combination of these things?

THE GATE SWINGS OPEN

When these men were finally "released from the kennel" — old enough to make their own spiritual choices — their reaction was similar to that of my neighbor's dog Riley. They ran free like never before.

When the gate swings open, some people completely rebel against Christianity and seek other religions or no religion at all. But Edward and Andrew were like the people I wrote about in the grace chapters of *Kingdom Invaders* who generally believed in the God of the Bible. So instead of full rebellion against what they were taught growing up, they tended to "run free" with a perception of God that fit what they believed He should be. Their liberty was expressed in different ways, however.

Edward never walked away from his faith in Christ. He was one of those who knew the Gospel was truth and never wavered in his commitment. He even became a minister. But unfortunately, because of his rigid spiritual upbringing, Edward responded with what I call the "knee-jerk reaction syndrome." His sermons were infused with excessive amounts of grace; there was very little that he found objectionable in the behavior of a Christian, unless it was expressly written in black and white in the Bible. While this may sound good on the surface, I submit that there is something to be said for a certain amount of thoughtfully considered man-made rules. (More about that later.)

Andrew on the other hand, rebelled against Christianity for a number of years after becoming an adult. His belief that he was heading to hell for breaking man-made rules had an almost tragic impact on his life. His rebellion led to a bout with alcoholism that nearly destroyed his marriage. By the grace of God, someone came into his life to explain the truth about grace and Andrew now proclaims faith in Christ.

Sadly as he was telling me his story, Andrew had a beer in one hand, a cigar in the other, and was throwing in an occasional cuss word to emphasize his points. It appeared to me that he was still rebelling against the spirit of religion which told him that a wayward activity or two would lead him to hell. From my perspective, Andrew was continuing to practice several destructive behaviors that were not good for him and did not reflect well on the one he called his Savior and Lord.

As Paul wrote in 2 Corinthians 5:17: "Therefore, if anyone is in Christ, he is a new creation; the old has gone, the new has come!" Unfortunately, while Andrew claimed a commitment to Christ, there was an awful lot of "old" in his behavior that effectively veiled the "new" that should have been increasingly evident his life.

LIBERTY CONSTRAINED BY LOVE

As I began pondering the stories of these men and what I believed to be the negative ways they had responded to their individual backgrounds, I found myself wondering "who was right?" After all, the Bible doesn't specifically prohibit those behaviors that I had always thought were objectionable to God. Edward as a pastor didn't seem troubled by them to any great extent. And Andrew seemed to have not only accepted those things, but actually delighted in them. With that being said, I had little doubt that they were both true believers in Jesus.

In my research for this book, I came across many people who practiced their liberty in Christ in ways that troubled me. So I found myself impaled on the horns of a dilemma. I knew that following a list of "dos" and "don'ts" didn't necessarily make you holy, but I was also sure that making holiness out to be unimportant wasn't right either. I believed that both perspectives needed to be given some credibility, although I was well aware of what the Bible says in Proverbs 15:9: "The Lord detests the way of the wicked but he loves those who pursue righteousness." So I struggled for a long time in finding proper perspective on the issue.

That was until I had a discussion with a woman I'll refer to as Natalie who grew up in one of those legalistic homes. For years, even after being out on her own, she felt trapped in the kennel of legalism. This kept Natalie fearful and unfulfilled in her Christian walk. Meanwhile, she had family members of the opposite perspective who seemed completely satisfied expressing their idea of freedom in Christ in unhealthy ways.

So for several years, she went through a similar dilemma to what I was facing at the time of our discussion. Although I had never felt trapped in legalism, Natalie and I did share the same uncertainty about what freedom in Christ really meant. We both wanted to please God with our lives, and encourage others to do the same, but were unsure of exactly how to do that.

Natalie told me all of that changed for her when she heard a sermon from her pastor on the subject. He rejected the bondage of legalism, but also said there were some prudent barriers that needed to be put in place in our lives. He called it "liberty constrained by love." When Natalie told me this, it was as if a veil was removed from my eyes. That was it! We have immeasurable freedom in Christ, but it all has to be practiced in the context of love — for ourselves, for our friends and loved ones, but most-importantly, for our God.

This was just like Riley as she was running free after her release from the kennel. When a vehicle approached, or some other danger lurked, I would call Riley to my side in concern for her safety — constraining her freedom for her own good in an expression of loving care. Similarly, while the founding fathers of my denomination did come up with a list of man-made rules that constrained some liberties, they were nonetheless intended for our own good as boundaries, or safeguards, against falling into sin. The problem came from the fact that too often the prudent constraint was enforced legalistically.

To help in understanding the difference between legalism and liberty constrained by love, I have come up with an analogy that relates to food. (I share many culinary analogies because I personally relate to them so well!)

Let's say there is a couple that forbids their children or anyone else who enters their home from eating breakfast foods at any other time of day except the morning. Eggs, bacon, sausage, waffles, and pancakes taste just as good no matter when you eat them, and they have the same amount of calories and nutrition in the afternoon and evening. So when asked why they have such a rule, the couple simply says: "Breakfast food is only to be eaten in the morning." No reasonable explanation is given; it is just a belief they have which is not supported by any legitimate facts. This would be an example of legalism.

Now let's say the same couple, under the same circumstances, made the same request based on a recent study. Researchers had discovered that people who regularly consumed eggs, bacon, sausage, waffles, and pancakes after noon were 33 percent more likely to suffer a heart attack before the age of 60. In this case, the couple had a very good reason for restricting the consumption of breakfast by their children and guests to the morning hours only – it was out of a valid concern for their well-being. This would be an example of liberty constrained by love. (By the way, don't worry. This was only a hypothetical study.)

In 1 Corinthians 6:12 Paul writes: "'Everything is permissible for me' — but not everything is beneficial." The second part of this analogy is a perfect example of that. Each person had the freedom to eat the breakfast foods whenever they wanted to; no one would have stopped them. But in the long run, doing so would not have been good for their lives.

I remember a pastor one time saying that, when considering *essential* things such as salvation through Jesus alone, we as Christians should have unity. In *non-essential* things, such as those not specifically addressed in Scripture, he said we should have freedom. And in *all* things, we should have love.

I agreed with two out of his three assessments. But in regard to non-essential things, I would say it is more important to emphasize *consecration* as opposed to *freedom* so that we can make sure to represent Christ well in all things. As it says in 1 Peter 2:16: "Live as free men, but do not use your freedom as a cover-up for evil; live as servants of God."

"RULE" HAS BECOME A FOUR-LETTER WORD

During my lifetime, the phrase "four-letter word" has been used to describe certain language that would not be used in polite company. More often than not, of course, it consists of curse words that are literally four letters long. Unfortunately, for many Christians today "rule" is looked at not only as a literal, but also a figurative, four-letter word. After all, as I've already mentioned, man-made rules can be a serious detriment to a healthy Christian life. In fact they can even create the exact opposite of the intended effect, causing people to tragically reject God for eternity.

But they can also provide a positive benefit, adding a layer of protection from the sins that can be very devastating to us or those we care about. So how can we know the difference between when rules are good and when they are bad?

One very negative aspect of man-made rules is that sometimes they are used as a substitute for true holiness. The Pharisees were a prime example of this. These Jewish teachers of the law were good at keeping and enforcing rules in public, but Jesus saved some of his strongest criticism for them. In Matthew 23:27-28, He called the Pharisees "whitewashed tombs" because they had all the outward expressions of righteous spirituality but on the inside were full of "hypocrisy and wickedness." The Pharisees had a respected public persona, but inside were judgmental and self-righteous.

Unfortunately, this is the way some people continue to express their spirituality. Edward experienced this in his life growing up. His parents put great emphasis on keeping the rules, but as I already stated, they were harsh, critical, and overbearing. Based on the people I have talked to, that was not entirely uncommon among those who grew up in Christian homes in the late twentieth century.

This is likely a major reason that *rule* has become a "four-letter word" among so many Christians today. In increasing measure, I have heard the establishment of any rules in a church or denomination spoken of very negatively, even from behind many pulpits. It appears again to be an example of the knee-jerk reaction syndrome. Rules were emphasized so much in previous generations that now they are being demonized (pardon the expression) as nothing but negative.

A MOVIE MISCONCEPTION

As an example, early in the establishment of the holiness denomination that I belong to there were stipulations against such things as going to movies. By the time I was a teenager my parents allowed me to go to movies, but in their generation it was widely forbidden.

Our founding fathers have been regularly belittled for introducing such a prohibition, particularly because of the comparative purity of the classic old movies of that time. However, there is a little known fact about the early days of film-making that may be hard to believe – but it is true.

As the infant motion picture industry began to grow up during the "roaring" 1920's, many Hollywood movies were actually becoming racy even by today's standards. This included graphic depictions of nudity, violence, cross-dressing, and homosexuality. The spiritual darkness in the heart of man has regularly been expressed throughout history through various forms of art, and filmmakers in the 1920's were no different. It was during this period that the leaders of many denominations called for rules prohibiting their members from attending movie theaters. (Keep in mind, there was no television or any other home viewing option available at that time.)

By 1930 the film industry was learning of dissatisfaction in Washington D.C. with the immoral trend in their movies, so the major studios began a process of self-regulating before Congress got involved. In 1934 the president of the Motion Pictures Distributors Association of America, William Hays, created the Motion Picture Production Code. According to *filmratings.com*, the so-called "Hays Code" consisted of an extensive set of moral guidelines that were strictly enforced into the 1960's. This is why virtually every movie you see from that golden era of film happens to be family-friendly.

Interestingly, my mom said her family avoided movies not so much because they were sinful, but because her parents didn't want to support the immoral Hollywood lifestyles with their money. Again, the darkness of the heart of man was evident as fame and fortune corrupted even some of the legendary Hollywood actors and actresses of that time. It is rare that the biographies of early film stars don't reveal lives of immorality and great contention.

In 1966 Jack Valenti was appointed president of what was now called the Motion Picture Association of America. Valenti considered the Hays Code an out of date form of censorship, so an early version of the rating system we use today was developed and implemented in 1968. As a result, movies with graphic depictions of sex or violence could now be legally produced and distributed — but at least the public would be warned before inadvertently viewing offensive content.

Those kids who were prevented from viewing movies during that previous 34-year period of relative purity eventually became adults. Not knowing the reason for the original prohibition, many who would call themselves Christians today have responded to the seemingly unnecessary, legalistic rule they grew up with by knee-jerking in an unhealthy direction. In many cases they are watching movies today that clearly *are* immoral and contain very objectionable subject matter.

Conversely, going to some movies in recent years has actually been a way for Christians to *support* their beliefs.

High-quality films with moral and godly content produced by devout believers have been increasingly making to the big screen with critical acclaim and large audiences.

A CAFFEINE CONCERN

There was also a caffeine prohibition instituted by several holiness denominations in the early 1900's, and in modern days there has been some knee-jerking going on here as well. Now be assured, I'm not casting any stones. I generally enjoy two cups of coffee each morning at work. But the overall consumption of caffeinated beverages has skyrocketed to an unhealthy level today, even among many Christians.

According to a Johns Hopkins University study from September 2013, "caffeine is the most commonly used drug in the world." The U.S. Food and Drug Administration says a healthy adult can safely handle up to 400 milligrams of caffeine a day. But beyond that, the study says there can be negative, if not dangerous, effects. These can include anything from nervousness and insomnia to cardiovascular issues and pregnancy complications. These symptoms are often evidence of caffeine intoxication, which is actually recognized by the American Psychiatric Association as a clinical syndrome.

It really doesn't take a lot to get to an unsafe level of caffeine consumption. For perspective on how much 400 milligrams is, the study says that a single medium-sized coffee at a typical coffeehouse can contain more than 300 milligrams. And most 16-ounce energy drinks will get you about halfway to the daily maximum, containing anywhere from 160 to 240 milligrams. With all of this in mind, it appears the founding fathers of these denominations may have had wisdom beyond their generation when they encouraged people to avoid caffeine.

Today the past man-made restrictions, such as those relating to movies and caffeine, may seem to be obvious examples of legalism. But they do serve to make the noble intentions of our denominational founders very clear — a desire to lead their people in carefully consecrating their lives and their bodies to God.

SAFETY, NOT SALVATION

So having man-made rules to follow isn't always a bad thing. After all, we have no problem with the establishment of rules in order to be part of a club. These rules help members understand what is expected of them in their conduct. And in another example, we generally understand that the multiple rules posted on the wall of an indoor pool — shower before entering the pool, no running, no diving, etc. — are there for our safety and protection.

It reminds me of a school many years ago that decided to get rid of the fence that surrounded its playground. The administrators arbitrarily decided the barrier made the children feel like they were imprisoned. This ended up creating an unpredicted and interesting phenomenon. Before the fence was removed, the children would regularly play throughout the playground right up to the edge of the property. But once it was eliminated, the kids subconsciously moved dozens of feet closer to the middle of the playground, not utilizing the areas near where the fence formerly stood. It was determined that before it was removed, the children felt safety thanks to the boundary that existed for their protection. When the fence wasn't there, they lost that sense of security.

This is similar to prudent rules that are established as a barrier of protection from spiritual danger. Rather than creating a legalistic prison, they actually enhance our freedom in Christ. The problem develops when these same rules are considered to be absolutely necessary for salvation. That is like the New Testament believers in Galatia who were returning to the centuries-old practice of observing the Old Testament law in order to provide for their own salvation. Paul wrote to correct this error in Galatians 3:2-3:

> I would like to learn just one thing from you: Did you receive the Spirit by observing the law, or by believing what you heard? Are you so foolish? After beginning with the Spirit, are you now trying to attain your goal by human effort?

This was the problem the previously-mentioned Andrew faced growing up. Whether it was his perception, or was incorrectly taught to him, Andrew truly believed that breaking certain man-made rules would send him to hell. Can you imagine the terror this could bring to a young child? Obviously I believe in teaching the full counsel of God, but we have to make sure that what we teach *is* the counsel of God, and not some personal belief that doesn't line up with Scripture.

So when discussing rules that are man-made and not actual commandments of God, it is very important there are no misunderstandings. Rules should not be used to somehow establish our spirituality, gain favor with God, or be "good enough" for salvation. Rather, they should be used prudently to create boundaries or safeguards against falling into sin. After all, no matter how strong a brother or sister in Christ may be, you will never find anyone who is completely insulated from temptations and vulnerability to sin.

As an example, there are many Christian ministries — *Family Life* and *Focus on the Family* among them — that have a prohibition against male and female employees who are not married to one another traveling, meeting, or eating together alone. It is often called the "Billy Graham Rule" because it was first implemented by the famous evangelist for members of his ministry team in 1948.

Does the Bible say, "thou shalt not travel, meet, or eat ye male and female employees alone one with another"? Of course not. But because of prudence and an understanding of our sinful natures, these organizations established (dare I call them) rules prohibiting such activity.

For the same reason, I say putting certain rules and boundaries in place is a wise thing to do in our individual lives, and in the lives of those whom God has placed in our care. So I have no problem with rules encouraging people to avoid vices such as alcohol and gambling. It's all about practicing liberty constrained by love as a way of keeping Satan at bay. (We'll look at these issues more in later chapters.)

CONCLUDING THOUGHT

It can be quite difficult to put a proper balance on the issue of man-made rules. Overemphasizing them is a bad thing, but considering them to be unimportant is also not good. Perhaps you've heard it said, "Rules without relationship leads to rebellion." I believe this is an accurate statement. Legalism occurs when rules are established and enforced at the whim of man without legitimate reason. But when rules are created with a love-based spiritual goal in mind, and that goal is carefully explained and understood, then their prudence is rarely questioned.

As in the examples I've already given, when rules are coldly given and enforced — whether it be with children or immature believers in Jesus — they can be used by Satan to create significant confusion at best, and serious rebellion at worst, with implications that can even be eternal. On the other hand, the parents of some of the most godly children I know were among those who took the time to lovingly explain their wise, reality-based concerns. Their kids were able to understand that the rules were there as an extra layer of spiritual protection, and rebellion was not an issue.

As this book continues, you will see that I have a similar goal. Just as these children have grown up to lead godly, spiritually productive lives, so too it is my desire that everyone who reads through these pages will learn important insights into the temporal and eternal value of radical devotion to God, even as it pertains to certain extra-biblical rules. Some of what I share will no doubt be met with resistance. But it is my prayer that as you read you will see it is all about a heart-felt concern for the spiritual protection of my brothers and sisters in Christ.

2–LIBERTY AND LOVE

Rather than judgmental, self-righteous, or legalistic condemnation that repels people, we need to carefully reach out with loving instruction and/or correction that will draw people to Christ, nurturing in them a desire to use their liberty as a reason to please Him and be more like Him.

In recent years I have become more and more aware of what I believe to be a supernatural, satanic strategy for making Christianity irrelevant and impotent in our culture. One aspect of that has to do with the changing mindset of believers, beginning with the idea that certain expressions of consecration are ridiculous. This has moved to a belief that anything short of full acceptance of worldly behavior is prudish and self-righteous. But the late Pastor Dr. D. James Kennedy put it very well when he said, "Jesus didn't call us to be the sugar of the world, He called us to be the salt of the earth." Because of the recent shift from "salt" to "sugar," there is regularly no discernible difference today between those who would call themselves Christians and those who do not.

It is often stated that expressions of love or kindness are what make the difference, and this certainly should be evident in the lives of those who believe in Jesus. But I have also been the beneficiary of a great deal of loving kindness from many unbelievers in my lifetime, so there has to be more to it than that.

Could it be that the choices we make, about what to partake of and participate in, really do matter? We have been led by many who would call themselves Christians today to believe that it doesn't make any difference. But the result of this misguided thinking is becoming increasingly evident in our churches, and subsequently in our culture, as the moral decay has accelerated in recent days.

PUTTING PROPER PERSPECTIVE ON RULES

As I mentioned in the previous chapter, the word *rule* has taken on a very negative connotation in modern Christianity. But as I also said, I think it has gotten a bit of a bum rap.

Perhaps the clearest illustration I can draw for you relating to rules in the Christian life would correlate to sports. In every form of competition, rules have been established for how to play the game. Some of the rules are firm and non-negotiable. Others are left more to the discretion of the officials.

Let's look at football specifically. An offense of 11 players is given up to four chances, called downs, to advance the ball 10 yards against an opposing defense. If they succeed, the offense gets a new set of downs in their quest to move the ball down the field. In order to score, the offense must get the ball into the end zone, or a kicker must boot the ball between the goal posts. These are among the firm and non-negotiable rules.

Since I first started watching football in the 1970's, the leaders of the league have altered some of the rules for the protection of the players. It used to be acceptable to almost kill the quarterback. Now the rules prohibit things such as helmet-to-helmet contact with the quarterback, tackling him at the knees, or driving him forcefully into the ground.

Other significant rule changes have affected receivers. When a player was catching a pass from the quarterback, it used to be fine for a defender to hit him as hard as he could anywhere on his body, to either knock the ball loose or send

17

him to the ground. The rules have now been amended so that hitting a "defenseless" receiver in the head, or with an abandon that would likely cause injury, are no longer permitted. These would be among the rules left to the discretion of the officials.

This example can be taken a step further by looking at my sports passion, NHL hockey. I love everything about professional hockey, including the amazing speed and finesse of the game. But I also enjoy the checking, fighting, and other violence — all of those things that will not be a part of our eternity in heaven. That's why I figure I'll have to enjoy it while I can! (Of course I have often wondered if it is OK for me as a Christian to enjoy something that is at its very best when contention is at its absolute worst — but that's an issue for another time.)

By the way, if you're not a hockey fan and wonder why they allow fighting in the NHL, I'll explain. Imagine you're a small kid in school and a big bully is picking on you. Before long another big guy comes along, not to bully you, but to protect you. The big guy fights the bully so he no longer bothers you. That is one of the main purposes of fighting in hockey — to allow the smaller skilled players to do their thing without fear of attack by the other team's "bullies." The fighters are commonly called "enforcers" because they enforce an unwritten code of conduct on the ice so the violence doesn't get out of hand. As a formerly small kid who occasionally got bullied, I love this part of hockey!

OK, back to the real reason for including hockey in this discussion. As with football, there are firm and non-negotiable rules. Among them — the puck must cross the opponent's blue line prior to the attacking team entering the offensive zone, and the puck must completely cross the goal line in order to score.

But the other rules in the NHL, such as what qualifies as a penalty, have gone through more changes in recent years than the color on a chameleon. The league expansion in 1967, which doubled the number of teams, led to a watering down of the talent pool. As a result, less-talented players were doing an increased amount of hooking, holding, and interference in order to compete with the more skilled players.

The referees were lax with enforcement of these rules, perhaps at league direction, which added to the entertaining contention of the games. But by the 1990's the less-skilled players were becoming bigger and somewhat faster, and defensive systems were increasingly sophisticated. This combination resulted in a game that became plodding, and at times boring, as scoring opportunities became rarer and rarer.

A labor dispute in 2005 led to a canceled season and an opportunity to do a redirection in the enforcement of the rules. The next season the referees were told to call penalties to the letter of the rulebook. The result — the NHL once again became the most exciting sports league in the world (author's opinion) and the fans loved the fast-paced, wide open game. Even the enforcers had to be talented hockey players or they weren't able to be competitive on the ice.

When the "negotiable" rules left to the discretion of the officials were previously considered unimportant, the talented players were not able to live up to their potential and the league as a whole suffered the consequences. When these rules were deemed to be essential for success, and were enforced as originally intended, the integrity of the sport was reestablished and the entire league and its fans were the beneficiaries.

Similarly, I would submit that there are regularly great benefits to Christians who consider certain man-made rules to be important. Rather than stifle our freedom in Christ, these guidelines can actually unshackle us to fulfill our potential as God's servants.

When it comes to our lives as Christians, there are rules — or commandments — written in the Bible that are firm and non-negotiable. The most famous would be the Ten Commandments, which tell us among other things that it is sinful to murder, commit adultery, steal, lie, or disobey our parents. But the negotiable rules would include some of the things I've already touched on such as those addressing drinking and gambling.

So how should we handle these negotiable, or man-made rules? I believe using the "liberty constrained by love" approach that I introduced in the last chapter is the best way to deal with this question. And as I pondered what to use for an appropriate analogy, the activity of dancing seemed to provide just the example I needed.

THE DANCING DILEMMA

Perhaps you came from a background in which dancing was commonplace. But if you are like me, you came from a denomination in which the founding fathers considered dancing a forbidden activity.

Of course, dancing has been around for several thousand years — pretty much since God created man — and at times has been a rather sensuous activity. In an Old Testament example, the Hebrew people became very sinful while Moses was up on Mount Sinai in Exodus 32. When Moses finally came down from the mountain, verse 19 says he saw an idol the people had made and "the dancing." In verse 25 it says the people were "running wild" and "out of control." From these words it can be assumed with virtual certainty that the dancing was not pure and pleasing to the Lord.

In the New Testament, the daughter of Herodius danced before Herod on his birthday in Mark 6. It says in verse 22 that her dancing "pleased Herod" and he promised to give her anything she wanted, up to half of his kingdom. I would venture a guess and say a dance that prompted such a response was likely, again, far from pure and pleasing to the Lord. So this type of activity has always been around, but in the United States it is a rather recent phenomenon that sensual forms of dancing have become accepted by society as a whole, and even by many Christians.

Once more, I believe this is the result of a knee-jerk reaction. For much of the twentieth century, denominations like mine prohibited dancing. Now, a few short decades later, dancing is almost glorified among Christians as the ultimate expression of freedom in Christ. Even our worship songs today speak regularly about dancing. So we have seen a clear move on this issue from the realm of perceived legalism to liberty.

Now before we go any further, I'd like to clarify some things. First of all, we have to acknowledge that the word "dancing" actually means many things. It is similar to the word "love" in that there is a continuum of very good to very bad in explaining its meaning. The word love is used to describe the perfect agape love of God on one end, to the completely immoral action of an unmarried couple "making love" on the other end. In between would be the romantic love we have for a spouse, the powerful love that a parent has for a child, or the so-called "love" we might have for a chocolate bar or some other favorite culinary treat.

Similarly, dancing can mean anything from a pure, worshipful expression on one end of the continuum — such as is found in Psalms 30:11, 149:3, and 150:4 — to something as provocative and sensual as pole dancing on the other end. In between would be such things as the healthy exercise of aerobic dancing, the fun of competitive dancing at a local school, or the loving warmth of a dance between a husband and wife.

So while there are many positive expressions of dancing, it's the negative that led the early leaders of my holiness denomination to decide it should be avoided almost entirely. Now that most forms of modern dancing have found acceptability with a majority of Christians, looking at the issue through the lens of "liberty constrained by love" is quite timely.

THE WEDDING NIGHT

Wedding dances are pretty much commonplace today no matter which denomination you belong to. Of course when I was growing up, our churches didn't have dances. We would have wedding receptions where we would eat good food, rejoice with the newly-married couple while family and friends shared a few humorous and/or heartfelt comments, and maybe enjoy some creative games. And we were actually able to do a little catching up with relatives we perhaps hadn't seen in a long time without having to shout over loud music. I had no feeling that I was missing out on anything. Everybody left with smiles on their faces, with no reason for regret.

As I've grown older and wedding dances have become more acceptable among virtually all denominations, I have now been to many of them. There have been a few where I would have to say nothing objectionable happened. People had a lot of fun and the behavior remained God-honoring. This usually occurred because the music was family-friendly, if not Christian, and no alcohol was served. But a significant number of the dances have made me feel uncomfortable because of certain things that happened.

I realize my standards may not mesh completely with yours, but there are some things as brothers and sisters in Christ that we should be able to agree on. Seductive body movements are clearly something that we should detest as dishonoring to God. Any man reading this, if he is honest, would have to admit that certain movements by a woman on the dance floor can be extremely tantalizing (consider the response of Herod to the dance of Herodius). I won't expound on this anymore because this is a family-friendly book, but it doesn't take much imagination to know what I'm talking about. So liberty constrained by love would dictate that great care should be taken with how we dance, particularly the ladies, because men are more visually oriented.

VENUES OF CONCERN

What about dancing at venues such as nightclubs and bars? I've heard the case made by some Christians that the activity they themselves participate in is not sinful so they have no problem going to such places. But I would urge anybody who makes this a practice to consider certain things. Perhaps *your* activity is not overtly sinful, but what is going on around you? Sensual dancing, excessive alcohol consumption, music with graphic lyrics — these are all common at nightclubs and bars.

Do you really want to support such activity with your finances? And are you sure that this activity is not having a negative spiritual impact on the friends and/or family that accompanied you there? If you are honest with yourself, are you sure that none of this activity creates a temptation for you? Are you in effect endorsing sinful activity by your presence there? And would it bring any disrepute to your Lord if someone were to see you at such a place?

Liberty constrained by love for your friends and/or family would probably mean a different form of entertainment would be spiritually safer and less prone to leading a weaker brother or sister in Christ to stumble. And what about unsaved friends or family? Clearly nothing in a place like that would give them a desire to turn from a life of sin toward the salvation available through Jesus.

When considering liberty constrained by love for your God, it would likely mean you would rather spend your money on a more wholesome activity that would please Him. You would want to flee the temptation inherent in such a place, and associate yourself with a more righteous atmosphere preventing any appearance of evil.

THE EXTRA SAFE, EXTRA MILE

Another thing that should be of concern is dancing that takes place between unmarried couples. It has always been a mystery to me as to why it is OK to physically touch and stand in such close proximity to someone who is not our spouse just because music is playing. Can you imagine being in the parking lot after the dance is over, holding that person in a typical dance position while rehashing the events of the evening and saying goodbye? That would be absurd! There is an intimacy to this type of physical behavior that gives Satan opportunity to create temptation.

For those who say I'm being ridiculous, I encourage you to be completely honest with yourself. Have you ever experienced a romantic or even sexual vibe when dancing with someone who is not your spouse? If your answer is yes, then you have felt the powers of darkness seizing the moment in an attempt to bring destruction upon your life. Liberty constrained by love would say you need to go the extra mile to protect your marriage — or your purity if you're single.

In the excellent 2008 Sherwood Pictures movie *Fireproof,* Kirk Cameron stars as Caleb, a fireman who experiences serious marital problems before God heals his relationship with his wife Catherine. Near the end of the movie, when the couple is reconciling, they give each other a rather intimate hug and kiss. The only problem is, the actress who plays Catherine is not Kirk's real-life wife. So the Christian producers of the movie had his actual wife Chelsea flown in and carefully hid her identity in the film so Kirk would be hugging and kissing her, not the other actress. The producers did not have a huge budget to make this movie by any stretch of the imagination, but they felt it was worth the cost to bring Chelsea to the set just for that scene.

Of course Hollywood and the rest of the secular world would say that's ridiculous — "just kiss the other actress, it's no big deal." But these Christian movie makers, and Kirk, felt like it was worth the extra cost to prevent any potential temptations and negative ramifications to his marriage. Similarly, I would submit that it is worth going the extra mile to protect our marriages, including the choice to dance only with our own spouses.

LOSS OF INNOCENCE

As adults have been losing any spiritually-based reservations about dancing in the culture, it has had an obvious effect on our children. Across the nation, there have been numerous reports in recent years of high school dances becoming very difficult for administrators to control. Certain types of dancing have been practiced that are so graphic they almost seem to be a type of foreplay. New rules have had to be enacted by many school districts in an attempt to rein in the sensuous behavior.

And I know I'm not going to win any popularity contests with what I'm about to say, but I think it's worth taking a little time to discuss something that is quite iconic in American culture. High school proms used to have a certain air of innocence, creating fond memories to be cherished. But memories for today's students often involve regret and shame. Sadly, there is much surrounding contemporary proms to be concerned about. The event is looked at as merely the "pregame" by many participants who expect a great deal from their date after the dance is over. And the prom dresses have gotten much more expensive, while the amount of fabric in them has decreased significantly. The common frame of mind today is, "if it isn't sexy, then it isn't a very good prom dress."

There is also a lot of partying and drinking associated with most proms once they get beyond the supervision of the school. As a Christian, whether you are a parent or a student, liberty constrained by love for your God would dictate that maybe it's time to take a second look at whether or not these types of school dances should warrant your endorsement or participation.

For the student, Paul gives a great admonition in 1 Timothy 4:12: "Don't let anyone look down on you because you are young, but set an example for the believers in speech, in life, in love, in faith and in purity." So no matter what your age, God's light can clearly shine through you. In fact, because behavior is far more likely to be driven by unwise impulses during the teen years, this is an age in which a godly, self-controlled life would point even more dramatically to the transforming power of the Holy Spirit.

When the founding fathers of my denomination prohibited dancing, I believe they had a foresight into what would happen someday. The activity has proven it can go very easily from something that is acceptable, too questionable, to downright sinful. So perhaps we need to show a measure of grace to those anti-dancing proponents of the past. It's agreed they likely went farther than they should have in their broad-stroke prohibitions of dancing. But as I've mentioned before, for them it was a case of wanting to radically consecrate their lives to God while encouraging others to do the same.

One final thought on the subject. When I was in high school, our church youth group used to have what we called "senior banquets" that were an alternative to the prom. We would invite a date, get all dressed up, have a great meal and presentation, maybe go bowling or some other fun activity, and everybody had a wonderful time. As I recall we even had a progressive dinner or two in which we would go from house to house for each of the courses of a meal. It was a blast! These were very memorable events that glorified God and we all left with no regrets. This is the type of thing I would endorse wholeheartedly and would encourage youth pastors to consider sponsoring in the future.

Admittedly, this dancing discussion has become a rather lengthy example of how liberty constrained by love should be our guide in how we live our lives as Christians. But this is a vitally important conversation because it's an approach that really applies to just about everything we choose to participate in or partake of. And this will be the foundation of much of what is discussed through the remainder of this book as we learn how to defeat Satan through lives of radical devotion to God.

CONCLUDING THOUGHT

As I have made my thoughts known to friends and loved ones on the prudence of constraining some of our liberty as Christians, it has been amazing to me how many people have said: "But it is not up to us to dictate to others how they should live their lives; we should just let the Holy Spirit do the work." I agree with that to a certain extent. The Holy Spirit *is* the One who convinces people of their sin and convicts them when they do wrong. But God also regularly chooses to use His people in advancing His purposes. If this wasn't true, then why would we be encouraged to stand in the gap and pray for brothers and sisters in Christ who are facing a crisis? After all, God already knows their needs.

And why would God establish the ministry gifts of apostle, prophet, evangelist, pastor, and teacher if we weren't expected to actively disciple others toward a greater consecration to the Lord? If the Holy Spirit was supposed to do all the work without our involvement, then why wouldn't we just stop teaching and preaching? And why would it be necessary to witness to the unsaved about our faith? After all, the Holy Spirit would lead people to repentance and reveal all things in due time to bring sanctification in the life of a believer.

The fact of the matter is God wants to use *us* as His vessels to reach unbelievers, and to help other believers grow in their sanctification. We are expected to do our best, pray that it's blessed, and the Holy Spirit will take care of the rest. Where we as Christians have fallen short many times is the way we accomplish that mission. Rather than judgmental, self-righteous, or legalistic condemnation that repels people, we need to carefully reach out with loving instruction and/or correction that will draw people to Christ, nurturing in them a desire to use their liberty as a reason to please Him and be more like Him.

3-RESIDUAL EFFECTS: FROM THE CULTURE

The choices we make as Christians — for better or for worse — regularly have a residual effect on others. We can never assume that what we do, or don't do, has no impact beyond ourselves.

Is looking different as a believer in Jesus really that important? As I pondered this question, a curious phrase kept coming into my mind: Residual effects. Granted, these are peculiar words to think about in relation to such a question. But hopefully things will become clearer in just a few moments.

There are many things in life that leave a residue — some for the good, some for the bad. For example, most commercial car washes these days have a cycle that leaves a wax residue on your vehicle. This protects the finish from the sun's damaging rays in the summer and the salt that is used to de-ice the roads in the winter. This is a *good* residual effect. Conversely, the salt that is applied to roads to make driving less treacherous, when mixed with the thawed ice, leaves a residue on vehicles that will eat away at the finish and rust the underlying metal over time. This is a *bad* residual effect. Bringing this discussion full circle, I believe our lives as Christians also have a residual effect for good or for bad.

It reminds me of when I first got my driver's license. The freedom I felt with that new privilege was awesome, but I also soon became aware of the immense responsibility that came with that freedom.

One day I was running a little late for work and I was admittedly driving too fast considering the heavy traffic on the city streets at the time. I was preparing to make a dangerous move to pass a car in front of me. I was too close to the car to be safe, and all of a sudden the driver hit the brakes hard to avoid a bus that pulled out in front of her. I did not have time to react and rear-ended the car. In the vehicle along with the woman who was driving were her two young daughters. By the grace of God, no one was hurt. But it was a sobering realization that I literally had the ability to destroy lives if I didn't make the choice to keep the good of others in mind while driving.

Similarly, the choices we make as Christians — for better or for worse — regularly have a residual effect on others. We can never assume that what we do, or don't do, has no impact beyond ourselves. That is the main reason I decided to get specific about certain attitudes, actions, and activities that we, in my belief, have become a little too comfortable with as Christians. These are the "gray areas" that don't necessarily have chapter and verse in the Bible to directly condemn them, but because of their ability to be used by Satan to destroy lives I felt it was very important to address them.

In the next two chapters I will give several examples of residual effects that have had a negative overall impact on the Kingdom of God, including many friends and loved ones whom we love and care about. In the subsequent chapters I will highlight the positive residual effects that we can have as we choose to be salt and light in the culture. I will reiterate once again that I understand you may have significant disagreements with my arguments. But please don't get upset with me. Let's just be praying together, seeking the Lord's heart on these matters, with the goal of pleasing Him first and foremost on our minds.

PULLED BY POTTER, SHAPED BY SHACK

The first example of a negative residual effect I would like to address has to do with the Harry Potter phenomenon. (I wrote about this in more depth in *Kingdom Invaders*.) Many Christian parents I have talked to say they have no problem with the book series and subsequent movies because their kids read the books with no apparent side effects.

This is not a surprise, because even though a May 2006 Barna Group study found that a significant number of young people wanted to learn more about Witchcraft as a result of their exposure to the Harry Potter chronicles, it was still a small minority — about one in eight. Yet, considering the potential eternal implications, that sounds a little like spiritual "Russian Roulette" to me — firing a gun at your head because only one of the chambers in the weapon has a bullet in it.

I believe if you look at the evidence with an open mind, the spiritually dark residual effect of the Harry Potter phenomenon in the United States has been undeniable. When I wrote *Kingdom Invaders*, I quoted a statistic showing that, at the very least, there had been a three-fold increase in the estimated number of people practicing Witchcraft since the series captivated the nation beginning in 1999. In 2007, that number had reached as many as 600,000. As I sought out further statistics for this book, I found the troubling growth of Witchcraft had not waned — actually far from it. I was shocked to learn that a Pew Research Center study in 2014 estimated the number of professed witches in the U.S. had grown to 1.5 million!

I don't believe it is a coincidence that this exponential growth has occurred since Harry Potter hit the collective consciousness of the nation. And please remember that these are not just mere statistics, but rather, souls that are now more likely to end up in a hopeless eternity in hell. Is it really worth the potential spiritual risk?

There is a more recent book that has also been controversial among Christians. It entered my radar because, at the time of this writing, a motion picture was about to be released based on the book. *The Shack*[3] by William Paul Young has been both endorsed and vilified by very prominent, respected Christian leaders. You can put me in the category of those who reject the book because of the negative residual effects it has created since its release. It had sold some 25 million copies as of 2018. And who knows how many people have read each copy of the book? There is no question it has had a tremendous opportunity to influence tens of millions of people with its message.

For those unfamiliar with the story, the main character, Mack, has to grapple with the death of his young daughter who was abducted and sexually assaulted before being murdered. The story centers on God reaching out to Mack to promote the healing of his devastated heart.

Sounds like a good redemptive message, right? And there is certain theology in the book that I do agree with, including God's unconditional love and the critical need for true forgiveness. These are among the reasons the book has been embraced by many sincere Christians. But unfortunately, Young doesn't stop there.

It's hard to quantify the impact of the book because this is not as tangible through statistical evidence. But I will examine with you what has happened in the realm of Christian thought in the decade-plus since *The Shack* was written. I have seen a lot of commentary on the very many theological problems with the book and subsequent movie — some more troubling than others — but I'm just going to focus on the few that in my opinion are the most dangerous.

REJECTING RULES, CANCELING COMMANDS

Earlier, I commented that *rule* has become almost a curse word in Christianity. In chapter 14 of *The Shack*, Young completely dismantles the notion that a believer in Jesus should concern himself with keeping any rules, including clearly written biblical instruction such as the Ten Commandments themselves. On page 202 the main character Mack asks Sarayu, who is supposed to represent the Holy Spirit, "...why did you give us those commandments?" Sarayu responds, "Actually, we wanted you to give up trying to be righteous on your own. It was a mirror to reveal just how filthy your face gets when you live independently."

Really? The Ten Commandments were written so we can give up trying to be righteous on our own? These foundational precepts of God certainly reveal our inability to live perfectly holy lives, but did He really write them (and repeat them in both Exodus and Deuteronomy) because He wants us to give up our personal attempts to live righteously? The residual effect of such a message should be clear — that not only are man-made rules to be rejected, but we must now also consider the direct commands of God in Scripture to be optional.

This dangerous false teaching is addressed directly and unambiguously in 1 John 2:3-5:

> We know that we have come to know him if we obey his commands. The man who says "I know him," but does not do what he commands is a liar, and the truth is not in him. But if anyone obeys his word, God's love is truly made complete in him.

In other words, those who say they are Christians but don't make the choice to obey God's commands are not telling the truth about what they believe. These are not my words, but the words of God — available for all to see — in Scripture.

I think the previous excerpt from *The Shack* is very helpful in understanding why the book is so endorsed by some solid Christians, and so vilified by others. If you are a well-grounded, mature believer in Jesus, you understand that we indeed cannot live righteously without help from the Holy Spirit — and that is perhaps the way you received what was written by Mr. Young. But what about the millions of unsaved people and immature believers who read this believing it to be actual truth from God? They just heard that rules and righteousness aren't important. If we can't live righteously on our own, then why even try? This is why I often repeat that what we *say* as believers, especially those who are Christian leaders, is not as important as what people *hear*.

I believe *The Shack* also resonates with those who grew up in legalistic "Christian" homes where keeping rules was harshly enforced while the love of God was not properly displayed. Young's words on page 203 would speak to those damaged by this type of upbringing. Mack says to Sarayu, "Are you saying I don't have to follow the rules?" The response: "Yes. In Jesus you are not under any law. All things are lawful."

Now, the mature Christian is likely going to understand this to mean that a relationship with God is more important than keeping the rules. This is *good*. But what is the average, less-than-mature Christian reader going to get from this? Likely they will be receiving it just as written, "...I don't have to follow the rules" and "all things are lawful." This is *not good*.

This thought is reiterated one more time on the same page when Mack responds to Sarayu by saying, "Are you telling me that responsibility and expectation are just another form of rules we are no longer under?" And the God character, Papa (who is portrayed as a large African-American woman for most of the book), responds simply, "Yup." However, this is quite contradictory to what is found in John 14:23-24:

Jesus replied, "If anyone loves me, he will obey my teaching. My Father will love him, and we will come to him and make our home with him. He who does not love me will not obey my teaching."

As I said, it's hard to know how much influence *The Shack* has actually had. But could it be that the image of God created by William Paul Young has played a role in the prominent "Grace Gone Wild" beliefs that I wrote about in *Kingdom Invaders*? The Church today has become so wrapped up in the perfect love and grace of God that is has largely forgotten about the fact that He is also a God of perfect justice, holding us accountable for our disobedience to Him.

UNDENIABLE UNIVERSALISM

There is also the issue of Universalism that is clearly promoted by Young in *The Shack*. Also called universal reconciliation, Universalism is the belief that everyone will be going to heaven regardless of their spiritual beliefs or how they had lived their lives.

In chapter 11, "Here Come Da Judge," Young takes 19 pages to make his case that God would never allow anyone to go to hell. Mack finds himself with a beautiful, omniscient woman in a cavern of judgment. Talking of God on page 162, the woman says to Mack:

"You believe he will condemn most to an eternity of torment, away from his presence and apart from his love. Is that not true?"

"I suppose I do."

The woman then tells Mack that he must send three of his five children to hell, and it is up to him to decide which ones. Mack fights against this until finally, he cries out, "Please, let me go for my children, please..."

This is represented as the immense love of Jesus who died on a cross for mankind. This is *good*. But the broader message is that, just as Mack couldn't bear to send any of his kids to hell, certainly God loves everyone too much to allow anyone to go to such a place of eternal torment. This is *not good*, because it is not biblical. Jesus Himself says in Luke 12:4-5:

I tell you, my friends, do not be afraid of those who kill the body and after that can do no more. But I will show you whom you should fear: Fear him who, after the killing of the body, has the power to throw you into hell. Yes, I tell you, fear him.

So my question to you is this: Should we trust in what Young *believes* about hell, or what Jesus *knows* about hell?

Later in *The Shack*, Papa (as a reminder, this is the father god figure in the book) says to Mack on page 192:

"Honey, you asked me what Jesus accomplished on the cross; so now listen to me carefully: through his death and resurrection, I am now fully reconciled to the world."

"The whole world? You mean those who believe in you, right?"

"The whole world, Mack."

But this is simply not compatible with what the Bible says in John 3:36: "Whoever believes in the Son has eternal life, but whoever rejects the Son will not see life, for God's wrath remains on him." So again, are we supposed to believe in William Paul Young's version of spiritual reality, or what the timeless word of God says?

For those who still aren't convinced that Universalism is promoted in *The Shack,* a more recent book written by Young, *The Lies We Believe About God,*[4] should remove any doubt about his understanding of this eternal-life-threatening belief. In an excerpt from chapter 13, Young writes:

"God does not wait for my choice and then 'save me.' God has acted decisively and universally for all human-kind. Now our daily choice is to either grow and partici-pate in that reality or continue to live in the blindness of our own independence...Here's the truth: every person who has ever been conceived was included in the death, burial, resurrection, and ascension of Jesus."

And Young apparently anticipated the questions of stunned readers when he added the following words, just to remove any doubts about his belief on the subject:

"Are you suggesting that everyone is saved? That you believe in universal salvation? That is exactly what I am saying!"

Knowing clearly what Young believes about Universalism, it should be seen as absolute vindication for those of us who have long sounded a warning about that message in *The Shack*. It would be completely unreasonable to believe that Young was not trying to promote that message in the book since we now know it is his firmly held belief.

I truly believe the ensuing residual effect has been an accel-erated acceptance of Universalist theology among those who call themselves Christians since *The Shack* was released. It has become a huge issue. Tens of millions of people have been able to receive this false teaching into their hearts and minds through the vehicle of a compelling, emotionally gripping story. Is it just a coincidence that Universalism is no longer just a fringe belief in Christianity but is now receiving mainstream acceptance? I don't think so.

A TRANSGENDER GOD?

One issue I haven't made a big deal about, but I believe deserves a mention, is Young's portrayal of God as a woman. There is a good reason given for this characterization in *The*

Shack — that Mack couldn't deal with God as a father figure because his own dad was so abusive. But to me this is still not acceptable.

For one thing, what impact is God portrayed as a woman having on those who are experiencing gender confusion? The sexual identity issue has become a significant problem in recent days. And while I certainly don't believe this is a direct result of *The Shack,* I would be pretty confident in saying that the growing acceptance of transgenderism among Christians is, at least in part, a residual effect of the tens of millions who have read the book or viewed the movie.

And try to put yourself in the place of the gender-confused individual for a moment. If God can change *His* gender identity to suit His desires and will, why shouldn't *I* be able to do the same?

Please remember, God created people male and female (Genesis 1:27). He had no confusion when He formed each of us in our mothers' wombs and it is ludicrous to even imply that He could make such a foundational mistake as to mix up our gender. Can you imagine God having to sheepishly say, "Oops, my bad!" Me neither.

No one is born the wrong sex. Statistics show that a person with gender identity issues has usually faced some sort of trauma that brought them to that place. So remember, they need our compassion, not ridicule or judgment. Just like anyone else caught in a satanic deception, we need to love them with the love of Christ so they can find the healing they need through Him.

Just for the record, I understand that there are those born in our sin-sick world who have certain sexual anomalies. For example, a chromosomal abnormality in males causes a disorder called Klinefelter Syndrome. Those who are born with this affliction have certain less-than-masculine physical traits. Still, this in no way provides proof that someone could be born the wrong sex. In fact, the symptoms of Klinefelter Syndrome can be minimized through medical treatments such as testosterone replacement therapy — proof that it is a disorder, not an issue of sexual identity.

Satan certainly understands that God is to be viewed as a father. This is why there has been an intensifying spiritual battle in recent years to diminish the importance and role of the father in families. If a man can be seen as weak, unintelligent, irresponsible, selfish, neglectful, abusive, etc., then confusion can be created in the proper understanding of God the Father.

To me this subject is really a no-brainer. Although God is spirit, whenever a gender is mentioned in the Bible He is *always* identified as male. I have heard it said a time or two that God shouldn't be considered only male because He created women too — therefore He certainly has female qualities as well. I simply respond to that by pointing out that I have long eyelashes, beautiful strong finger nails, am very sensitive to the point that I cry easily, and I've never seen a Hallmark Christmas movie that I didn't like. These are all considered largely female attributes, and yet I am fully man through and through.

But the strongest argument for God's gender identity is the fact that Jesus, God incarnate, was a man's man. He was able to withstand a brutality before His crucifixion that I don't think many of us men could have survived. It's possible that most of us would have never made it to the cross. To me this is case-closed, smoking-gun evidence that the understanding of God as male should be embraced, not questioned.

A personal, true-to-life example of this particular concern I have with *The Shack* actually reared its ugly head during a discussion I had with a young man while writing this chapter of the book. The conversation began at a pizza-on-a-stick booth at our State Fair when this individual saw a political button I was wearing. The candidate I supported was a Bible-believing Christian, and after the man asked me a question about him he made a derogatory comment about my support for him. I said, "Why do you say that?" He told me that he was an ultra-liberal and proceeded to say that this is America and "shouldn't we be free to do whatever we want?"

Just so you know, this man was in no mood for a cordial dialogue. I believe he was *trying* to portray himself as interested in a sincere debate, but he couldn't help but get loud and somewhat bullying in his approach.

In response to his question, I told him I am a Christian and that I believe our freedoms have to be practiced in obedience to God's commands in the Bible. I barely got the words out of my mouth when he blurted out, "I'm a Christian too. In fact I have a minor in theology!"

"Then you know that God says in His word..."

He interrupted me before I could finish my sentence (which was common throughout our conversation)..."Why do you keep referring to God as male?"

"Because the Bible calls Him our heavenly Fath..."

"Of course you know the Bible was written by homophobic men!"

"Well, actually, it was written through men by the Holy Spirit..."

"That's not true."

Again, the young man didn't wait for my response when he blurted out, "Don't you think that I or anybody else should be able to love whoever we want to love?" This question was clearly in reference to homosexuality, and it gave me insight into his vitriol against me and my biblical beliefs.

I responded, "Well, we as Christians are supposed to obey the commands of God. And in the Bible, from Genesis to Revelation, God's design for sexuality is clearly spelled out

– only within the bonds of marriage between one man and one woman. Even Jesus affirmed this design in Scripture." (That's found in Matthew 7). I was thankful that for some reason he let me complete my thought on this very important point.

He then proceeded to call into question the reputation of Jesus. "Nothing is said in the Bible about Jesus' life from the age of 12 to about 27 or 28." (It was actually about 30.) "What do you suppose He was doing during those years?"

I was about to answer that He was learning and growing while preparing for the most important responsibility ever given to anyone in the history of the world, but the young man didn't give me a chance... "During those years Jesus was doing 'very human things.'" Of course, his implication was that Jesus was sinfully sowing His wild oats.

I said, "That couldn't be true because the Bible tells us that Jesus had to be sinless..."

When he interrupted this thought he almost made my point for me..."You have slept around [not true] and I have slept around, so none of us is sinless..."

I was excited that these words came out of his mouth, and *I* may have actually interrupted *him* at this point... "That's exactly right. And that is why Jesus had to die for us. His sacrifice wouldn't have meant a thing if He had sinned even once – the Bible tells us that."

The young man may have felt at this point that he was losing the argument so he shifted back to his original debate tactic – bringing God's gender identity into question. "Did you know that God is an African-American female?" I wasn't sure why he referred to this bazaar portrayal of God as found in *The Shack*, but I wasn't going to bite. I had felt good about where the Holy Spirit led our conversation and decided it was time to bring it to an end. I told the young man the food we just bought was getting cold and we weren't going to change each others' minds anyway so we might as well just conclude our discussion. I thanked him and began to walk away.

He apparently felt as if he had not properly put me in my place. As I turned my back he yelled out something about being an American and included some gross profanity. A couple of women standing there looked me in the eye as I began to walk past them as if to say, "What is his problem?" I smiled at them and turned to the young man, asking him politely to take it easy. Apparently he then realized the inappropriate nature of his behavior and language. As I resumed my departure, he feigned regret and apologized to the women with animated emotion while simultaneously blaming me for his outburst.

It occurred to me that our conversation revealed further evidence of a negative residual effect of *The Shack*. As gender fluidity is placed upon God in the book and movie, it is happily being used as an example for those who want support for an "anything goes" sexuality. As Christians, we are doing absolutely nothing good when we choose to somehow intellectualize the issue – perhaps saying that God is spirit and therefore neither male nor female, or that females were created by God and therefore He is somehow also female, or whatever other supposedly enlightened logic is used.

It should be clear from my conversation at the State Fair that *The Shack* is one weapon Satan is using to advance a perversion of God's design, physically and sexually. As Christians, let's just focus on scriptural reality: The Bible calls God our heavenly *Father*; and Jesus, God incarnate, was not only all God but also all *man*.

There is absolutely no reference in the Bible to Jesus forsaking His masculinity. Unquestionably, He had a tender, sensitive heart. But this is no different from the nature of millions of men — now and throughout history. That doesn't make them any less male. When discussing this issue, we should simply focus on the unambiguous description of God that we find in the Bible, and leave no room for any misinterpretations that could be used against His design and plan for men and women.

PAST PERCEPTIONS

As I've mentioned several times already, our pasts play a significant role in how we view things. This includes how we interpret what we hear, see, or read. It has been my observation that those who wholeheartedly endorse *The Shack* regularly came from backgrounds of pain related to Christianity, such as children from homes where an unhealthy, mortal fear of God was used by parents as a tool for discipline, or where legalistic rule-keeping was deemed more important than loving nurture in the faith.

Others have been hurt as adults by self-proclaimed Christians who said or did painful things, maybe through self-righteous, judgmental comments or very ungodly behavior. By the way, this is another example of a negative residual effect — that sometimes a proper understanding of Christianity can be skewed by the inappropriate way it is represented by self-proclaimed followers of Jesus. Young himself came from such a background, which included incidents of sexual abuse, and it appears from his writings that he is trying to make Christianity into what he thinks it should be as opposed to what it really is based on God's Word.

INFLUENTIAL FICTION

One final thought on the subject of *The Shack*. Its defenders will often say it is "just fiction" so why are we making such a big deal out of it? But fiction has proven to be a very effective tool for transmitting a message. An example would be the 1950 book, *Dianetics, the Modern Science of Mental Health*.[5] Its author was L. Ron Hubbard, a science fiction writer. Hubbard's made-up, fictional philosophy sounded so good to so many that a whole false religion was started based on the book. And today, Scientology is leading millions on a path to eternal death. Conversely, Jesus used many parables — or fictional stories — to send powerful, positive messages that lead to eternal life. So clearly, works of fiction cannot always be considered inconsequential.

I have also heard some proponents of *The Shack* say that other books and movies present a religious worldview that is opposed to Christianity so why aren't we making a big deal about them? This would include, for example, the *Star Wars* phenomenon. Among other things it has frequent instances of communication with the dead, and the ever-present activity of "The Force." These concepts are found woven into the tapestry of Eastern religions such as Hinduism, Buddhism, and Shintoism. And the second film that was released, *The Empire Strikes Back* (20th Century Fox, 1980), practically contains a tutorial on Eastern mysticism when Yoda is training Luke Skywalker on a planet in the Dagoba system.

Now, I have been captivated by the *Star Wars* movies as much as anyone else. But one might be left to wonder if there has been an undeniable residual effect here as well. Nearly everyone in the nation has seen at least one of the movies, and Eastern religions have gained widespread, mainstream acceptance in our culture since the *Star Wars* phenomenon began in the late 1970's. I can recall as a teenager trying to manipulate The Force after seeing the early movies. For me, coming from a Christian home, it was just a temporary curiosity. But how many spiritual seekers have been drawn to this enticing concept thanks to *Star Wars* and have spent a lifetime influenced by the mystical aspects of Eastern religions?

But there is still a distinct and important difference between *The Shack* and other books and movies with religious implications. *Star Wars* and the like don't pretend to be speaking for the God of the Bible, or as God. *The Shack* clearly *is* presenting itself as speaking from God's perspective, going so far as to create a "holy trinity." I don't believe there is any question that this has had the residual effect of blurring the line of spiritual reality for a significant number of readers and viewers. Sadly, a great number of these people are either completely or somewhat biblically illiterate — even many who would call themselves Christians — and they are accepting Young's skewed version of "truth" rather than the timeless and absolute truth found in God's Word.

THE DUNGEONS AND DRAGONS DECEPTION

There is one final cultural phenomenon that I would like to address before bringing this chapter to a close. A role-playing game that became popular in the early 1980's deserves mention here as well because I believe it too is having a negative residual effect — first on the culture, and now in the Church.

Dungeons and Dragons was almost universally recognized by Christians at that time as a dangerous introduction to the occult and was largely avoided. It featured demons, witches, spells, magic, and curses. The object was to kill your enemies before they kill you, all in a quest for wealth and power. In those days there were numerous suicides, and even murders, that were committed by those who were found during investigation to be devout players of the game.

In 1985, the weekly TV magazine show *60 Minutes* investigated the reports of more than two dozen deaths purported to be related to *Dungeons and Dragons* and found the link to be undeniable. Evidence included suicide notes referring to the game, and *Dungeons and Dragons* paraphernalia near the bodies. There were calls by loved ones left behind, including the parents of dead teenagers, for a ban on *Dungeons and Dragons*. But for various reasons, including the threat of lawsuits, the game remained on the retail market.

Things had been pretty quiet related to *Dungeons and Dragons* since then, perhaps because of the publicity surrounding the related deaths. But in recent days, its popularity has been seeing a resurgence thanks largely to the availability of internet competition. Only this time around, *Dungeons and Dragons* is not being played by just non-believers; it is also being embraced by many Christians. This is following the same pattern I have seen with so many practices that at one time were understood to be spiritually dangerous.

My question to the participants would be this: Why would we as Christians want to introduce something like this into our own lives or the lives of those in our spiritual charge such as our kids or fellow church members? Shouldn't we be able to agree that anything which utilizes demons, witches, spells, magic, and curses as an avenue to entertainment should not be considered good, clean, harmless fun?

The residual effect of our endorsement as Christians should be clear. It is not a trivial number of parents who, over the last several decades, are still grieving the loss of their children thanks to the devastating effects of this "harmless" game. Through *Dungeons and Dragons* the powers of darkness have been allowed a foot in the door to wreak havoc in the lives of a significant number of participants and the result too often has been death — both temporally, and sadly, eternally. Do we as Christians really want to give something like this our stamp of approval?

CONCLUDING THOUGHT

I would ask you to consider once again the fact that so much of what we do as Christians has a residual effect, for better or for worse. As we continue looking at this principle in the coming pages, I want to warn you — I have only begun to mettle! When you care about someone, you are concerned about every aspect of their lives. And when you see them participating in something that has great potential for harm, you will certainly want to make your opinion known to them.

That is my sole purpose for addressing these topics. My heart hurts as I have seen more and more of my brothers and sisters in Christ falling for what I believe to be a great deception — that their questionable attitudes, actions, and activities don't matter. But a plethora of statistics back my assertion that these behaviors, including the many gray areas we will soon be discussing, are indeed dangerous on both physical and spiritual levels.

Please keep reading the following chapters with an open mind. If I deal with something that you are personally participating in, I would simply ask that you consider my arguments and then pray that God will give you direction. After all, if it is truly your desire to please Him I know you will certainly want to understand His heart on these matters.

4-RESIDUAL EFFECTS: FROM THE CHURCH

Sadly, today there are literally millions of people who are on the everlasting "road that leads to destruction" while they are being taught in their churches that everything is OK. This is despite the fact that their choice to continue practicing sinful behavior, whatever it is, is condemned in black and white in the Bible.

When discussing the residual effects you get from the culture, as we did in the last chapter, you expect that most of them would be negative. But when it comes to residual effects from the Church, you would certainly hope that these would all be positive. Unfortunately, this is simply not the case.

There have been periods of Church apostasy in the past which thankfully were met by resistance among some courageous ministry leaders — and the result brought important reformation. But the apostasy, or falling away from biblical truth, seems to be very different today. Things within the Church appear to be irreversibly falling in line with the end times prophecies found in Scripture.

In Matthew 24:10-11, Jesus Himself made it clear that apostasy would be a foremost sign of the last days. He stated that "many will turn away from the faith" due to deception from a significant number of "false prophets." I believe the false prophets spoken of in this passage could include many pastors of our present age who are widely respected, among even mature believers, due to the perceived successes of their "mega" churches. But sadly, interspersed with some good teaching have been messages that subtly but dangerously stray from biblical truth.

Is this intentional on their part? I can't answer that. One thing I do know is that the more influential these leaders become, the more Satan is going to try and bring confusion to them and their messages. As their churches multiply — and they write books that are sold in the millions, are interviewed in various forms of media, and as other prominent people and organizations seek them out for advice and direction — this can be very pride inducing. And pride is a powerful tool in Satan's toolbox for bringing disrepute to the message and/or messenger of the Gospel.

DOES "MEGA" MEAN MATURITY?

Some people make the argument that it is OK if the message is a little off at these mega churches because, "look at how many people are being saved." Dozens, if not hundreds, come forward to accept Jesus as their Savior every week, and the Kingdom of God appears to grow. But the problem comes from the fact that a significant number of these people want Jesus as their *Savior*, without a commitment to making Him their *Lord*. One of these prominent mega church pastors is famous for telling people that all they have to do is believe in Jesus, receive His love, and they are now part of the family of God. However, this positives-only, culturally-acceptable approach includes no mention of the need for repentance, or turning away from their sin.

Internal research done at one renowned mega church revealed a troubling lack of such spiritual maturity among its thousands of members. A 1996 survey of Pastor Bill Hybels' Willow Creek Church in Chicago revealed that 25% of singles, 38% of single parents, and 41% of divorced individuals

49

admitted to having illicit sexual relations in the previous six months.[6]

So one of God's unambiguous commands in Scripture — that sex is only to be enjoyed between one man and one woman within the context of their own marriage — was either not known, or was being intentionally ignored, by a significant percentage of the members of this church. And keep in mind, this wasn't after years of being beaten down by temptation or some other vulnerability. Nor was it a survey of any random six-month period over the course of several years. This was activity that occurred during the short six months prior to the survey! So it would be logical to assume that such immoral behavior had become routine in the lives of these members.

One is left to wonder how many other foundational biblical truths were deemed to be unimportant as evidenced by the way they lived their lives. Interestingly and sadly, Hybels resigned in April of 2018 due to several allegations of sexual impropriety against him that spanned several decades.

Therefore, the size of a church can't necessarily be equated with spiritual success. We shouldn't feel like we have to accept everything prominent pastors say just because the numbers appear to indicate they are being blessed by God. In some cases this is true, but in far too many cases it is not. A prophecy in 2 Timothy 4:3-4 reveals that in the last days many church leaders will willingly compromise the message of the Gospel as a way of pleasing people over God:

> For the time will come when men will not put up with sound doctrine. Instead, to suit their own desires, they will gather around them a great number of teachers to say what their itching ears want to hear. They will turn their ears away from the truth and turn aside to myths.

So if a pastor shares biblical truth that these people don't want to accept, they will move on to a church where the pastor does say what they want to hear. This would include some of the mega churches where the pastors, in many cases, grew their congregations on the strength of a compromised, more culturally-acceptable message.

As an example, the well-known pastor of one of America's largest churches never talks about the negative aspects of biblical truth, such as the need to live sacrificial lives for the cause of Christ, or the reality of an eternal hell for those who choose to reject God to the end. His message is basically that God always wants us to be healthy, wealthy, and wise. And if we're not there yet, we will be someday soon. When asked about this, he says that life today is so difficult and stressful for people that he just feels they need to hear an encouraging message from him week after week.

I find this to be a curious viewpoint. Does he really believe that life for the average Christian in the United States today is more difficult and stressful than it was for the first century believers? After all, the followers of Christ in New Testament times generally lived very hard lives, working sun up to sun down just to be able to feed their families. They regularly faced persecution, and many were even martyred for their faith. I could be wrong, but this sounds a lot more difficult and stressful than the existence of the average Christian in America today, a country where we have relative affluence and religious freedom.

It was in the midst of the unfriendly first century culture that believers in Jesus were taught the whole counsel of God, whether it was immediately uplifting or not, so these people could deal with the truth, the whole truth, and nothing but the truth. And the Church grew rapidly in size and influence as a result. They learned to cope with their difficult and stressful lives with an eternal perspective that came through true spiritual maturity. They knew that sometimes God would calm the storms of life, but other times He would merely hold onto them through the storms. This realistic understanding of the

Christian life is a valuable lesson that all believers need to be taught today.

Of course, the same pastor of this mega church has also authored numerous feel-good books that have sold millions. Despite all of this apparent success, it is likely a sad reality that most of the people who read the books, and perhaps a significant number of people who attend his church, aren't even aware of their need for a savior as a residual effect of the compromised, people-pleasing message he consistently shares.

I believe a microcosm of this "feel-good only" preaching philosophy can be seen in the way some churches conduct Communion today. When I was young, the Communion service was looked at as a sacred event. Special time was set aside during a Sunday morning worship service in reverence for this sacrament that was established by Jesus Himself at the Last Supper. Before we ate the bread and drank from the cup, the pastor would read from 1 Corinthians 11:23-26 so everyone would have a proper understanding of why we were doing what we were doing.

The passage concludes with the words: "For whenever you eat this bread and drink this cup, you proclaim the Lord's death until he comes." This necessarily means that the person taking Communion must be a Christian, because an unbeliever would have no anticipation of the eventual return of a man who died on a cross. The pastor would then continue reading perhaps the most important portion of this passage; verses 27-29:

> Therefore, whoever eats the bread or drinks the cup of the Lord in an unworthy manner will be guilty of sinning against the body and blood of the Lord. A man ought to examine himself before he eats of the bread and drinks of the cup. For anyone who eats and drinks without recognizing the body of the Lord eats and drinks judgment on himself.

So not only must Communion participants be Christians, but they also must first examine themselves. Is there sin in their lives? If so, they must confess this sin to the Lord and commit to repentance before partaking of the bread and the cup. Otherwise they "eat and drink judgment" on themselves.

Sadly, in so many of today's excessively grace-driven churches, this language — although straight from Scripture — is rarely if ever mentioned. The prevailing mindset is to avoid making anybody feel anything negative, so the decision has been made to just serve Communion to everybody; no profession of faith in Jesus is necessary. And of course, any talk of judgment is left out of the discussion as well. This is clearly in keeping with the comfort focused direction of so many of today's seeker-friendly churches.

With all of this being said, I want to make sure it is understood that there are also some very good mega churches in which the Gospel message is clearly shared and spiritual growth is encouraged on a weekly basis. One pastor friend of mine who leads a church of thousands regularly admonishes his congregation to dig in deeper with God, spending more time in prayer, worship, and Bible study. I have heard him say more than once from the pulpit that he doesn't want the church services to be just "theater Christianity," but rather, a place where people actively engage to become better equipped and more effective servants of God.

No matter where you currently make your church home, be it big or small, I encourage you to study the Bible daily while simultaneously praying that God will reveal His truth to you. That way, if a Christian leader is teaching something that does not line up with Scripture you have put up a guard that the Holy Spirit can use to protect you from being deceived.

THE YEARNING FOR YOGA

One method being used by many pastors today as a tool to grow their churches is yoga. The practice has rapidly become a cultural phenomenon and many pastors today are apparently seeing it as a way of popularizing their churches to the broader community. I addressed this issue at length in the first book in this series, *Kingdom Invaders*. It is perplexing to me that yoga is seeing such growing acceptance among so many Christians and their leaders.

Calling it "holy yoga" or "Christian yoga" doesn't change the fact that it was created by a Hindu guru for the sole purpose of uniting with their cosmic god of the universe — a step in the process of escaping the cycle of reincarnation. The guru who developed the practice, Patanjali, said that even the postures and focused breathing in yoga, which are largely defended by Christian practitioners as neutral, are spiritual expressions to clear the mind and prepare the body for meditation.

The late author and filmmaker Caryl Matrisciana was born and raised in India, ground zero for Hinduism. In a *Christ in Prophecy* TV broadcast from August 2011, Matrisciana said, "In Hindu teaching, it is known that there is no yoga without Hinduism and no Hinduism without yoga. The two cannot be separated."

In fact, the word yoga actually means "yolk or union" with god. But not the God of the Bible. It is a union with the Hindu's cosmic version of god. This is the reason I am so baffled as to why many churches are incorporating this practice into their outreaches. Why would we introduce our members and visitors to something carrying all of that occultic spiritual baggage? Is it about trying to become the most culturally relevant church in the community? And if so, at what cost?

I have heard some people testify to the "healing" aspects of yoga, including such things as the minimization or even elimination of chronic pain. These individuals will tell you that they swear by yoga as the reason for their return to a normal life. But can yoga really be given all the praise?

I recently suffered a herniated disk in my lower back which caused the worst pain I can ever remember in my life. Days and weeks passed where I couldn't get up out of bed, or off of a chair, or (pardon me) even use the bathroom without excruciating pain. Something as simple as getting in and out of my car was an adventure in pain. And dropping an item on the floor was cause for tears because there was no way to reach down and pick it up without agony.

But that began to change when I got an MRI and the problem was diagnosed. I was administered injections in my back to ease the pain, which allowed me to begin a process of physical therapy. Through several weeks of daily stretching and exercises, the muscles around my damaged disk were built up and the pain subsided to the point that I was able to function normally again. The modern physical therapy methods of good ol' stretching and exercise did the trick.

Let's say I am having this same issue with my back and someone suggests the practice of yoga as my route to pain relief. So in my desperation I take their advice. I do the stretching and postures that provide a boost to muscle tone and I start feeling relief over time. What is the result? I praise yoga as the answer to my suffering.

Now you might ask me, "If yoga and the physical therapy that you received have virtually the same function, then what is wrong with practicing yoga?" But even by asking the question there is an admission that there is something special to yoga beyond its physical exercise. With the mystical baggage I have already mentioned, wouldn't it be wise to seek out other forms of exercise and pain relief that don't invite potential spiritual danger?

This question is valid. One of the negative residual effects of the growing acceptance of yoga among Christians can be proven with empirical evidence. Chris Lawson is director of the Spiritual Research Network. In his July 2008 website article "Kundalini Energy: Yoga's Power, Influence and Occult Phenomena in the Church" Lawson wrote:

> "Whether one is just a beginner or an expert, all yoga postures and breath prayers have the capacity to invoke dark, evil powers. Involving oneself with yoga...and any form of kundalini energy arousal can lead to severe and prolonged bouts of demonic oppression, mental states of extreme depression and despondency, demonic entities influencing the human body, etc. I have personally seen and helped Christians that have been left in vegetable-like mental states and who have experienced undiagnosable excruciating pain."

Thankfully it is true that a significant majority of Christians do not experience such dramatic symptoms from their encounters with yoga. But it is also undeniably true that many do. And regardless of whether or not one can completely divorce the spiritual aspect from the beneficial exercise, what about others who are drawn to yoga by our endorsement as Christians? It is an extremely valid concern that these people could end up with a teacher — or in a setting — that makes no effort to guard against the mystical aspects of the practice which can open the door to demonic activity.

It should be no surprise that as the practice of yoga is becoming increasingly accepted in Christianity, another primary Hindu belief is also gaining legitimacy among believers. A Pew Forum on Religion & Life poll published in December 2009 found that 22 percent of professed Christians, more than one in five, accepted reincarnation as truth. More concerning in this poll was the fact that 10 percent of those who considered themselves to be evangelical Christians believed in reincarnation. And even among those who were considered "highly-committed" believers, attending church on a weekly basis, 5 percent believed in the legitimacy of reincarnation.

These poll results came despite the fact that reincarnation is in no way compatible with biblical truth. Reincarnation is the belief that after you die, you will be born again into a new life. That life will either be better or worse, depending on the karma you produced in the previous life. Karma has to do with good works and bad works. The more "good karma" you produce, the more likely the next life will be better on the way to uniting with the universal soul, or the cosmic god of the universe.

It should be noted that most Hindus also believe in transmigration. While reincarnation would dictate that humans return in the next life as another human, transmigration allows for those with very bad karma to return in other life forms such as bugs or animals.

These beliefs run completely counter to the foundational biblical teaching found in Ephesians 2:8-9: "For it is by grace you have been saved, through faith — and this not from yourselves, it is the gift of God — not by works, so that no one can boast." And in Hebrews 9:27 it says: "...man is destined to die once, and after that to face judgment."

That judgment is described in Revelation 20. Those who are not faithful to Jesus, and therefore their names are not found in the book of life, will be cast into hell for eternity. This is called the "second death." Of course the first death is the physical death we face on this earth. And that's it, a two death limit.

So based on Scripture, the belief in reincarnation has no basis. It is merely one more attempt by man to create a more favorable reality. If we didn't do well in one life, we have a chance to do better the next time around. And there is no hell to face for rejecting God to the end. Instead, by our own good works we can continue to progress to a better place. Sadly this is a fiction that an increasing number of Christians are beginning to accept with potentially eternal consequences.

The other residual effect I'd like to address relating to yoga is not quite as tangible, but is still very credible when considering biblical prophecy. In Revelation 17:1-18, an end times one-world religion is described as "the great prostitute." I don't believe it is in any way exaggeration to say that Satan is using the Hindu-origin practice of yoga as one of his tools in creating a widespread mindset that will have no trouble accepting a universal religion.

Do you doubt this? A rapidly growing number of self-proclaimed Christians today will tell you that sincere Hindus, or Buddhists, or Muslims, or whoever, will be going to heaven as long as their beliefs are sincere. Sadly, no matter how sincere their beliefs, the Bible tells us that their eternity will be in hell unless they accept Jesus as their Savior and Lord. As it says in John 3:16,18:

> For God so loved the world that he gave his one and only Son, that whoever believes in him shall not perish but have eternal life...Whoever believes in him is not condemned, but whoever does not believe stands condemned already because he has not believed in the name of God's one and only Son.

I would encourage you to read what I have just written about yoga one more time and then answer this question: "Why would we allow something that has such great potential for spiritual harm into our homes or churches?"

CONTRIBUTING TO A CRUMBLING FOUNDATION

One teaching that is gaining popularity in our churches, and is being championed by several high-profile Christian leaders, is clearly having some very negative residual effects. I'm not sure how long this particular belief has been around;

I personally have only been aware of it for a short time. If I knew about it when I wrote the first book in this series that was published in 2015, I probably would have included it as a key "Kingdom Invader" – I believe it is that spiritually dangerous.

It is called unofficially, or perhaps officially, the minimalist perspective. It starts with the assumption that in this modern age people think of the Bible merely as a compilation of ancient documents, so we shouldn't worry about making a case that it is inerrant and infallible. This perspective is driven by the belief that it is so hard to defend the unbelievable accounts in the Bible, such as the worldwide flood of Noah's time or the virgin birth of Jesus, that we shouldn't even try. Instead, let's just focus on the death and resurrection of Jesus because anyone who can die and then resurrect himself from the dead deserves to be heard and believed in.

One prominent pastor in particular says he no longer uses the words in his sermons "the Bible says" or "the Scriptures say" because too many people simply don't believe in the Bible as the authoritative Word of God anymore. If this is true, and it probably is, then I would say it is because an attack on the foundations of Christianity has been going on for a long time in our culture.

For example, there are many Christians, and even pastors, who are already bringing into question the authority of the Bible in its very first pages when they try to make the Genesis account of creation fit into the evolutionary model. The question of whether or not to take the Bible literally took on new life in the 1800's when Charles Darwin and the theory of evolution began to gain credibility in the scientific community of that day. Because his theories appeared to be based on science, many Christians started to feel that their Bible-based creation theology must either be flawed, or the result of misinterpretation.

So it was thought that in order for belief in Christianity to remain viable, evolutionary ideology had to be somehow integrated into the Bible's account of creation. Therefore, many Christian leaders over the years have been willing to accept — or have even advocated for — the so-called Gap Theory of creation, or the Day-Age Theory.

The Gap Theory allows for a gap of millions or billions of years in Genesis 1, between verses 2 and 3:

> Now the earth was formless and empty, darkness was over the surface of the deep, and the Spirit of God was hovering over the waters. And God said, "Let there be light," and there was light.

But when you read these verses without any preconceived ideas, and without the verse numbers included, it is very clear this is simply one continuous commentary. It's a real stretch to believe anything else.

The Day-Age Theory says that the six days of creation in the Bible are not actually literal days, but rather, periods of time. That way the creation process could have gone on for millions or billions of years. But again, if you take the Scriptures at face value as written, it becomes clear that the days of creation are literal twenty-four hour periods. In context with the rest of the Bible nothing else makes sense.

In Genesis 1:3-5, God himself established the concept of the twenty-four hour day when he separated light from darkness and called them "day" and "night." And the words, "there was evening, and there was morning – the first day" are used to complete the description of all six days of creation making it quite unreasonable to believe these were anything but literal twenty-four hour periods. (I address this topic more in depth in chapter two of *Kingdom Invaders*.)

THE BIBLE AS AN IDOL

So this is just one example of how the authority of the Scriptures is called into question — when we try to incorporate man's ideas into what the Bible actually says. And when this new breed of pastors says we shouldn't worry about defending the accuracy of the Bible, but instead focus just on Jesus and His resurrection, they are in essence hastening the erosion of the Church's foundation.

The pastor I have been talking about makes it clear at Christmas time that he doesn't think it is necessary to believe in the virgin birth of Jesus so long as you believe in His death and resurrection. Apparently, convincing people that a baby could be born to a woman who has never been with a man is too difficult. And yet, this same pastor will say without hesitation that we can believe that a man who was brutally beaten, tortured, and killed could rise from the dead after three days. Does anyone else see the contradiction here? And this is only the beginning.

There is a somewhat circular argument made by those who teach this minimalist belief that in effect works against them. The very Bible that it is not necessary to defend is virtually the only source for the truth they are attempting to convey about Jesus' death and resurrection. There are many extra-biblical texts that will testify to the fact that Jesus did live, was an extraordinarily influential figure, and died through crucifixion on a Roman cross.

But to my knowledge, the only documentation outside of the Scriptures testifying to the fact of a risen Jesus were written by a small number of additional believers; there was no secular authorship. Of course, when you think about it this makes perfect sense. After all, who of the more than 500 people who saw Jesus after He was raised to life again could possibly remain a non-believer?

So this minimalist teaching bases its one undeniable truth on "a compilation of ancient documents" that may or may not be factual and without error. It should be obvious that this is an argument based on a shaky foundation that will eventually crumble.

One high-profile Christian leader even went so far as to say that calling the Bible the foundation of our faith is idolatry. What? Isn't he aware of what the Scriptures say about the Word? In John 1 there is no room for doubt that Jesus and the Bible, which is God's Word, are inseparably linked. In verses 1, 2, 12, and 14 it says:

> In the beginning was the Word, and the Word was with God, and the Word was God. He was with God in the beginning...Yet to all who received him, to those who believed in his name, he gave the right to become children of God...The Word became flesh and made his dwelling among us.

So saying it is idolatry to call the Bible the foundation of our faith is hard to fathom. But maybe this effectively proves my point. This Christian leader either doesn't know what the Bible says, or doesn't take seriously what it says based on his own lack of belief in its authority.

UNIVERSAL APPLICATIONS

My personal introduction to the minimalist approach came when I got into a lengthy discussion with a woman I'll call Lona. This was after I had shared a teaching on the biblical perspective of submission in the home. She felt like I endorsed the mistreatment of women because I stood by verses in the Bible such as:

- Ephesians 5:22 — "Wives submit to your husbands as to the Lord."

- Colossians 3:18 — "Wives submit to your husbands, as is fitting in the Lord."

- 1 Peter 3:1-6 — "Wives, in the same way be submissive to your husbands..."

I had tried to explain that God's idea of submission has more to do with chain of command; it means a man has more responsibility toward God for what goes on in the home, not more in the way of privilege. But Lona responded that she would *never* marry a man who expected that she submit to his authority. With this I told her my main concern was not so much her ideas about submitting to her husband's authority, but rather, the more important question as to whether or not she was submitting to God's authority.

Lona then went on to tell me that she believed the verses I shared were only meant for the people living at the time they were written, and were not applicable today. She based this belief on a concept she was taught by her pastor called "universal applications," which very much comes from a minimalist perspective. Basically it means that we should base our beliefs only on some very narrow fundamental biblical truths such as "God will never leave nor forsake us" and "God is love."

I do agree to a certain extent with the universal applications approach. For example, there are many false teachings and obscure doctrines taught in some churches that are based on a single passage of Scripture. This would include 1 Corinthians 11:2-16 where women are instructed to cover their heads when they pray, and 1 Corinthians 14:34 where women are told they must remain silent in the church. Apparently when Paul was writing this letter to the believers at Corinth, the behavior of some women in the congregation was causing a distraction. So he dealt with that issue in the midst of his other instructions that were meant for the whole church. It should be understood that the guidance related to these women wasn't addressed to the greater body of Christ.

THE IMPLICATIONS OF INTERPRETATION

So how can we know the difference? Here is what I have been taught and believe to be the proper understanding of how to interpret applicable scriptures: If a command or instruction is given in the Old Testament, we can know it is applicable to us today if it is reiterated in the New Testament. And if it is in the New Testament, we can be assured it is timeless doctrine to follow if it receives repeated mention.

The point at which the universal applications approach becomes deeply troubling is when it is predictably taken too far. For example, there are many Christians today who believe homosexuality is an acceptable expression of sexual behavior because of the aforementioned universal truth that God is love. He would want us to follow through on whatever desires make us happy. This is despite the fact that Leviticus 18:22 and 20:13 say that homosexual behavior is "detestable." This is Old Testament so we have to take pause because we know that there are certain ceremonial and sacrificial laws, and certain harsh penalties for breaking such laws, that clearly don't apply to us today.

But the understanding that homosexual practice is an affront to God is reiterated in the New Testament repeatedly. In Romans 1:26-27 homosexuality is called variously, depending on the translation, a "perversion," "sin," or an "error," and a response to "shameful lusts." In 1 Corinthians 6:9-10 homosexual offenders are included among those who will not "inherit the Kingdom of God." And in 1 Timothy 1:8-10, those who practice homosexuality are listed among people described in the New Living Translation as "disobedient and rebellious," and "ungodly and sinful."

So the concept of universal applications, when defined too narrowly to beliefs such as "God is love," can be very dangerous — with possible eternal implications. If people are not taught that God is also a God of perfect justice, they won't understand that He will ultimately hold people accountable for their willful, unrepentant sin. As it says in Hebrews 10:26-27:

> If we deliberately keep on sinning after we have received the knowledge of the truth, no sacrifice for sins is left, but only a fearful expectation of judgment and of raging fire that will consume the enemies of God.

Sadly, today there are literally millions of people who are on the everlasting "road that leads to destruction" (Matthew 7:13-14) while they are being taught in their churches that everything is OK. This is despite the fact that their choice to continue practicing sinful behavior, whatever it is, is condemned in black and white in the Bible. (By the way, please don't have the misunderstanding that I hate those who practice homosexuality; I have only used this as an example. I always say that the most caring, loving, and compassionate thing we can do for them, or anyone else caught in a sinful lifestyle, is to share the truth in love.)

THE BIBLE BUFFET

A good general rule of thumb is this: Be wary of anything that gives permission to go against God's clearly expressed instructions in Scripture. A cartoon bubble comes into my mind when I hear people say they don't believe that certain precepts repeated several times in the Bible are for today. I can see God saying, "How many times do I have to put something into my Word before people will believe what I say and take it seriously?"

I have heard this type of thinking described as "buffet" Bible reading. Just as we pick and choose the foods that we like from a buffet table and leave the rest behind, some people choose to accept only those things in the Scriptures that they agree with while rejecting what they don't like. This is the undeniable, and I believe inevitable, residual effect of universal applications and the minimalist approach.

There are certainly instructions in the Bible that all of us from time to time will not want to accept (the stuff about loving my enemies and forgiving those who have hurt me are among my dislikes), but we don't have the option of making our own rules. If we try, it is to our own detriment — perhaps with eternal implications.

CONCLUDING THOUGHT

Barna's 2019 *State of the Bible* study found that nearly half of American adults — 48 percent — are now "Bible Disengaged," meaning they interact with God's Word infrequently, if at all. This is not surprising when you consider the false teachings being championed by many of our prominent Christian leaders today that completely dismantle scriptural authority.

I've said it before but it bears repeating. Anything we believe about anything is only opinion unless it's based on the Word of God. When we try to do things our own way, whether it be for personal accolades, perceived church growth, or whatever the reason — even when it may be with the best of intentions — the ultimate residual effect is always negative.

If it's apparent your church is moving away from its primary missions of disciplining its members in biblical truth and spreading the true Gospel of Jesus Christ; if the services, whether for youth or adults, seem more focused on entertaining than on godly worship and Bible teaching; and if small group gatherings prioritize fellowship and the latest cultural fads over digging into the Word of God for spiritual growth, then I would urge you to talk with the church leadership and lovingly but urgently encourage them to reconsider their direction. The stakes are just too high to consider the temporal, earthly successes of our churches more important than the eternal disposition of the many souls that God places in our care.

5–ATTITUDES:
OUTWARD EXPRESSIONS

*The attitudes, actions, and activities that are a part of who
we are as Christians go a long way toward either drawing
people to Jesus, or driving them away.*

A s I touched on previously, in my four-plus decades as
a Christian I had never really felt my spiritual beliefs
brought into question. While growing up in a Christian home
as part of a holiness denomination, I felt that what I was taught
was spot-on. But in recent years there were brothers and sisters
in Christ whom I respected that brought into question many
of the things I had always equated with righteousness. So that
began for me a personal search. James 1:22-24 says:

> Do not merely listen to the word, and so deceive your-
> selves. Do what it says. Anyone who listens to the word
> but does not do what it says is like a man who looks at
> his face in a mirror and, after looking at himself, goes
> away and immediately forgets what he looks like.

I began to ask the sincere question, "What should a Christian
look like?" This led to a serious study of Scripture and a daily
quest in prayer, asking the Lord to reveal His heart to me:
"What truly grieves You and what truly pleases You?" What
I felt God revealed to me went beyond my original question

dealing mainly with various activities, but extended also to attitudes and actions.

I am not expecting everybody who reads this to be in complete agreement with all of my conclusions because I will be dealing with many disputable matters, otherwise known as gray areas. All I ask is that you read with an open mind and be prayerful, allowing the Holy Spirit to speak His truth into your heart.

THE CASUAL CULTURE

Certainly, a lot of what I'm going to share is very counter-cultural, and even counter-Christian today. One thing I've noticed in our contemporary society is a casualness that has pervaded just about everything. I am a huge fan of the Minnesota State Fair, which is rivaled only by Texas as the largest in the nation. There is a history museum on the fairgrounds with photos dating back to the very beginning of the fair in the mid-1800's. I took note of the clothing that was being worn more than one hundred years ago around the turn of the twentieth century. The men were regularly dressed in suits and ties, while the women were wearing decorative hats and long dresses — and many were carrying parasols.

In comparison, as I walked out of the museum, I saw guys wearing shirts that often had vulgar comments on them, and many had "fashionable" torn pants. The women wore much the same thing, but were also quite prone to immodesty. And while I couldn't hear the conversations among the people in the old photos, I would imagine their language was laced with far less profanity than the typical conversations I overheard leaving the mouths of the modern fair-goers.

Similarly, I was recently reading a book written in conjunction with a legendary former player from "The State of Hockey." *Minnesota North Stars History and Memories with Lou Nanne*[7] provided an inside look at the franchise that Louie was part of as a player, coach, and general manager throughout its twenty-six years in the NHL. The book was filled with many photos dating back to the first game in 1967. Even that recently, the men who filled the arena were regularly dressed in suits and ties and the women were wearing dresses and skirts. While today's fan of the now Minnesota Wild is more likely to wear team logo apparel, the modern clothing is nonetheless far more casual.

THE CASUAL CHRISTIAN

This casualness has now invaded virtually every aspect of society, including the way many see their walk as Christians. We often talk proudly of how we can "come as we are" to our churches, wearing T-shirts, jeans, gym pants, shorts, flip flops, or whatever. While I can see some benefit to feeling comfortable in church, I do think there is tangible value in "dressing up" a bit. I often think that wearing nice clothing to church shows a visible measure of respect to God. We certainly wouldn't dress in our most casual duds if we were visiting the home of the president of the United States or some other dignitary. Why would we feel like God deserves any less honor in His "house"?

I believe without a doubt that the way we dress can have an impact on our mentality wherever we go. In my youth watching North Stars games, I can never recall seeing a nicely dressed individual in the arena getting drunk, throwing things on the ice, or yelling profanity. However, in more recent days I can recall numerous fans wearing the most casual of apparel getting thrown out of the games because of their inappropriate behavior. Obviously, the clothing doesn't dictate their actions. But think about this. When you are dressed in your finest clothing, maybe a suit and tie for men or a beautiful dress for women, doesn't it tend to affect your overall attitude? Doesn't it make you feel a little more sophisticated and perhaps somewhat better about yourself?

I know it impacts how people treat you. My oldest daughter worked for several years at a well-known clothing retailer and she bought numerous shirt and tie combinations as gifts for me that were very classy. During the spring and fall when the temperatures were just right, I would regularly dress up in these combos when I went to church. The reaction from people who I just met, or who didn't know me very well, was often quite interesting.

More than once I was asked if I was the pastor. Other times I would be invited into conversations about topics that were, unbeknownst to the other person, way over my head such as deep business or financial issues. Once, a woman even asked me when I was going to be taking over the radio ministry that I worked at, although I knew inside I would have been eminently unqualified for such responsibility at the time. But these comments I heard when I was all dressed up were truly a boost to my self-esteem. So the way we dress can have a great impact on the way we think, about ourselves and about others.

It has been my observation that the casualness of today's attire is merely symptomatic of the casual attitude that is pervading our culture today. And I truly believe this casual approach to life in general is now having a significant impact on how we view our walk as Christians.

LIVING WITH A HIGHER PURPOSE

As of this writing, I have been driving for about 40 years. I got into a few collisions when I was younger, which is typical of an inexperienced driver, but my last crash was now over 20 years ago (except for that suicidal deer that ran into the side of my car). I have also gotten only a single speeding ticket in all those years so I'm obviously not wild when I get behind the wheel. But there is one practice that has done more to make me a better driver than anything else — I began putting Christian bumper stickers on my vehicles.

I hadn't always been a fan of this particular way of declaring one's faith because I often thought the stickers were a little too in your face. I felt certain messages were well-meaning but could possibly repel a non-Christian, effectively accomplishing the opposite of the desired effect. But then one day I was perusing the retail tables at a men's Bible conference and saw a red bumper sticker with white letters that I just had to put on my car. It simply read, "Jesus is Lord."

I loved the fact that all I had to do was drive my car and I could make that heartfelt declaration about my beloved Savior to everybody who drove behind me. But it also became obvious to me very quickly that I was no longer representing only myself when I got behind the wheel. While I was already a generally courteous and law-abiding driver, I soon found out that I still had room for improvement. I could no longer angrily whip past another motorist going only 45 mph in a 55 zone, nor could I edge up to 10 mph over the speed limit when I was running late for an important appointment. I became very aware that my driving conduct could send a message about Christianity, either for good or bad.

If you can communicate that much without saying a word, you can imagine how much more important it is to represent Christ well in our everyday interactions with people. The attitudes, actions, and activities that are a part of who we are as Christians go a long way toward either drawing people to Jesus, or driving them away.

Eddie DeGarmo and the late Dana Key wrote a great song that was released in 1990 called "Casual Christian" (ForeFront Records) that was an anthem to the importance of living a committed life as a believer in Jesus. Among the lyrics:

This life is filled with strong distractions,
One pulls from the left, one from the right,
I've already made up my mind, I'm gonna leave this world behind,
I'm gonna make my life a living sacrifice

I don't want to be, I don't want to be a casual Christian

I don't want to live, I don't want to live a lukewarm life
'Cause I wanna light up the night with an everlasting light
I don't want to live a casual Christian life

The song eloquently stated that the way to allow our "everlasting light" to shine for Jesus is by giving our all for Him, making our time on earth a "living sacrifice," rather than carrying on a self-serving life that bears no eternal fruit for the Kingdom.

Sadly, the casual attitudes that have become prominent in our culture today have clearly impacted the way many believers in Jesus live out their everyday lives. For instance, I am troubled when I hear those who call themselves Christians say that they told somebody off when they felt they were wronged. People like telemarketers, customer service representatives, cashiers, and waiters and waitresses seem to be among the most vulnerable. The thinking seems to be, "I am justified in mistreating them because they interrupted my meal" or "the product I bought didn't work" or "I got bad service."

But how does Jesus feel about this? In Luke 6:27-28, 31-33 He says:

But I tell you who hear me: Love your enemies, do good to those who hate you, bless those who curse you, pray for those who mistreat you. Do to others as you would have them do to you. If you love those who love you, what credit is that to you? Even "sinners" love those who love them. And if you do good to those who are good to you, what credit is that to you? Even "sinners" do that.

The fact of the matter is, when we feel we are mistreated or taken advantage of — whether it's real or imagined — that's when our lights for Jesus can shine the brightest because we will respond in ways that are unusual to the world. But if we hold onto the belief that our rights have been violated and we would rather win an argument, we have just lost a golden opportunity to redeem that time for the Kingdom.

THEY ALL NEED THE LOVE OF CHRIST

I have heard brothers and sisters in Christ from time to time characterize their perceived offender as thoughtless, careless, lazy, stupid, etc. If this is truly the case, the fact of the matter is these people need Jesus as much or more than anybody. Just imagine, if somebody really does struggle with their intelligence, they likely have been mistreated all of their lives for their shortcomings. Wouldn't it be an act of incredible compassion to treat them with dignity and understanding when they make a mistake? And just imagine the message that is being sent to them about Christianity if a follower of Jesus shows them patience and kindness.

As 1 Peter 3:8-9 says:

Finally, all of you, live in harmony with one another; be sympathetic, love as brothers, be compassionate and humble. Do not repay evil with evil or insult with insult, but with blessing, because to this you were called so that you may inherit a blessing.

So we see here that a Christlike response to any perceived maltreatment really hinders any opportunity for Satan to wreak havoc. Instead of creating a potentially damaging witness to Christ, we instead have turned the situation around and created a blessing for that individual. And Peter says that *we* inherit a blessing as well.

This goes for any of these people we may have a complaint against. And I think it's important to add that this is where an incorrect judgment could be eternally devastating. The "thoughtless" offender could have a mind that is preoccupied with his teenager who was just hospitalized after a car accident. The "careless" waitress who spilled coffee on your

73

lap could be a single mom battling a medical condition that affects her coordination, but she's trying to support her two young children so she is continuing to work.

And I learned a lesson first-hand about showing telemarketers some respect. Working in non-profit Christian radio for most of my adult life has meant we have never had an overabundance of money as a family. So if my two daughters wanted to go to college, they knew they would have to pay their own way. When my oldest daughter left home to begin her college career, she ended up getting a job as a telemarketer. She worked at this particular company for about three years, putting up with the occasional nasty and even cruel remarks while she was responsibly paying for her college education.

That really helped put a human face on those telemarketers who would call just when I was putting a bite of food in my mouth, or during an important moment during the big game on TV. For one, they didn't know they were calling at a bad time. For another, instead of working for a living they could be doing something disreputable to obtain their money. But they have chosen to pay their bills by doing a job that is not glamorous and can have few rewards. Talking to them with dignity and respect, whether you feel like it or not, is a way of glorifying the Lord. And your kind conversation combined with a sincere "God bless you" before hanging up can literally give the Holy Spirit an opening to begin a work in their lives.

RESPECT IS NO RESPECTER OF PERSONS

Treating people with dignity and respect — regardless of how they treat us — gives God the opportunity to work in their lives. And it's very important that this attitude of respect begins at home. Colossians 3:18-21 says:

> Wives, submit to your husbands, as is fitting in the Lord.
> Husbands, love your wives and do not be harsh with
> them. Children, obey your parents in everything, for

this pleases the Lord. Fathers, do not embitter your children, or they will become discouraged.

This passage leaves no room for any disrespect in the home. God requires that husbands and wives show honor to each other, that kids show honor to their parents, and that even parents show honor to their children as the gifts from God that they are. As an attitude of respect fills the home, it nurtures the whole family in a godly atmosphere that limits the ability of Satan to cause damage in their individual lives.

This attitude of respect should also be exhibited as we leave our homes, such as when we go to school or our places of employment. In Colossians 3:22-23 Paul says:

> Slaves, obey your earthly masters in everything; and do it, not only when their eye is on you and to win their favor, but with sincerity of heart and reverence for the Lord. Whatever you do, work at it with all your heart, as working for the Lord, not for men...

When this passage of Scripture was written in the first century, slavery was an ingrained part of the culture. In the Roman-dominated world that Paul was a part of, about 50 percent of the citizens were slaves. But it wasn't slavery as we would understand it with our modern Western mindset. In the early years of Roman rule prior to the writings of Paul, brutality was an accepted part of the slave culture. This would have been similar to the shameful way a large number of slaves were treated in the southern United States back in the 1800's. But by the time of Paul, slavery for the most part had evolved into something more civil.

When the Romans would conquer a people group, they would enslave them; young and old, rich and poor, educated and non-educated. But rather than inflict severe hardship on them, most slaves would basically become a part of the family of the Roman citizens that purchased them. Their particular talents and abilities would be put to good use for the financial benefit of the slave owner. The slaves were treated much like children — part of the family but expected to be obedient to the masters of the house — and they would commonly receive an allowance.

After working for their owners for many years, these slaves would often have earned enough money to buy their freedom. But some would reject that opportunity because they didn't want to leave the family they had grown close to while working for them.

The oftentimes close relationships between first-century slaves and their owners can be seen in the account of the Roman centurion in Luke 7:1-10. This military man had a slave "who was sick and about to die." The passage says that the slave was valued so highly that the centurion asked Jesus to heal him. This certainly wouldn't have happened if the slave was just viewed as a mere commodity.

Obviously, those who used the Bible to condone the type of slavery that was largely practiced in the United States were in no way interpreting it correctly. It is indeed a blessing that God put it on the heart of President Abraham Lincoln, and a number of other courageous leaders, to make our nation one of the few in human history to put an end to slavery – even at the cost of a bloody civil war.

With the insight into ancient slavery, it is easier to put the passage from Colossians 3 into modern terms. We are simply being instructed to honor those for whom we are working. For students it is teachers, and for employees it is bosses. And keep in mind, this is not conditional on them actually deserving our respect. Just as with the Romans, often they do not earn the right to be honored. But verse 24 tells us that if we are obedient to God in this, "...you will receive an inheritance from the Lord as a reward. It is the Lord Christ you are serving."

Of course, in God's design this too goes both ways. Colossians 4:1 says: "Masters, provide for your slaves with what is right and fair, because you know that you also have a Master in heaven." So those who are business owners, bosses, supervisors, teachers — whatever the position of authority — you are instructed to treat those in your charge fairly.

Are you seeing a pattern here? An attitude of dignity and respect toward others is a universal requirement for Christians no matter who we are dealing with. Fathers, mothers, sons, daughters, male, female, teachers, students, employer, employee, rich, poor, white, people of color — you name it — we need to treat them honorably.

And keep in mind, there is no exception granted when it comes to social media. For some reason, people seem able to ramp up the nastiness when communicating online — this often includes Christians. I would encourage you before pushing the "send" button on any message to consider how it might be received by the person or people who will be reading it. Does the message honor God? Will it reflect well on your commitment to Christ because of its reasoned, thoughtful tone? Or will the message repel people from our Savior due to its angry, harsh, or perhaps hurtful words?

By the way, treating people honorably — whether online or in person — includes those who are advocating for things, or living in ways, we don't condone. Whether they are Christians or non-Christians, when they behave sinfully we should have an attitude of concern for their souls. We need to consistently love them the way God loves them. That way, when we are presented with an opportunity to share His truth with them, they will be more likely to listen to what we have to say knowing that we truly care about them.

CONCLUDING THOUGHT

When we respond to difficult people and situations in unexpected, Christlike ways we not only give God a chance to work in the lives of the offenders, but we are also given the promise in Luke 6:35 that our "reward will be great."

In 2 Peter 1:5-8 we are given a clear instruction:

...make every effort to add to your faith goodness; and to goodness, knowledge; and to knowledge, self-control; and to self-control, perseverance; and to perseverance, godliness; and to godliness, brotherly kindness; and to brotherly kindness, love. For if you possess these qualities in increasing measure, they will keep you from being ineffective and unproductive in your knowledge of our Lord Jesus Christ.

To use an unusual, but I believe highly appropriate word, it is our *peculiar* response to adversity that really grabs the attention of the unbeliever. When they see we have a peaceful attitude in the midst of trials, or that we are loving and kind even when mistreated, that's often when they begin to question why. That provides an opportunity to give them the answer: Our relationship with Jesus Christ. And then the stage has been set for us to be effective and productive vessels of service to God as we testify to His transforming power in our lives.

6–ATTITUDES:
THE SPIRIT WITHIN

If we have a reliably Christlike countenance we will provide the Holy Spirit with significant opportunities to touch lives for the Kingdom. People will be much more open to what we have to say. Otherwise, they will likely be repelled by our apparent hypocrisy.

In my adult life, when I wasn't in Christian radio I worked as a sheriff's dispatcher. That was a place where the effectiveness of biblical principles became glaringly obvious to me. When people would call in with a complaint, they were almost always mad at somebody; someone in their family, a friend, a neighbor, a deputy, or me — and they hadn't even met me! But in my eight years there, I could only remember a few times that I couldn't calm the complainant down before we hung up.

One time, deputies were responding to a domestic situation where an agitated man had assaulted his wife. He had been making his case to me on the phone before the deputies arrived to take him into custody. After the man was booked into jail, one of the deputies came to me and asked, "What did you say to that man before we got to the residence? We walked up to the door expecting a fight but he came out with his hands extended so we could handcuff him." All I had done was act out a biblical principle. I simply treated the man with dignity and respect — not because he earned it, but because he was a beloved creation of God despite his present behavior.

When you treat people with a Christlike attitude, it's amazing how often they respond positively. It doesn't work every time, but when it does you have just created a great opportunity to be heard. When they feel like you care about them as a person, they are more likely to be open to what you have to say. You could be just the light of hope they need in the midst of a painful trial, and that light is the reflection of Jesus that could change their lives for eternity.

There was another time when I was helping a neighbor lady move to a new house. I knew we needed more help but everybody I asked was either busy or out of town that weekend. (I know what you're thinking, but I did take their word for it). I had run out of almost all options until I thought about a man who recently started coming to our church. He was a baby Christian but had shown remarkable spiritual growth in a short time. Still, he was a tough-as-nails farmer who had a history of anger issues. But I felt I had no choice, so I asked him and he kindly obliged.

During the day, there were some rather irritating things that happened — furniture that wouldn't fit through doors, painfully crushed knuckles when we got too close to a wall with a heavy cabinet — you know, typical moving stuff. Despite my concerns, I was amazed at the farmer's reaction to the various difficulties we encountered. The fruit of the Spirit was already becoming evident in his life. He was patient, kind, and self-controlled. The woman knew where we went to church and I left feeling like we had witnessed to her, not only by serving her in a vital need that day, but also through the Christlike attitude exhibited by the farmer. (Maybe not so coincidentally, several years later that woman showed up at our church and became a regular attender.)

WINNING WHILE LOSING

Although I am saying we should reflect the fruit of the Spirit in our responses to difficult people and situations, I am not implying we should be doormats either. As an example, the driveway at our home out in the Minnesota countryside is about a tenth of a mile long, so when the winter snows come it is not practical to shovel by hand.

After we moved to the home in 1999, I had an agreement with my original plow guy in which I would call him each time we needed him to clear our driveway. He charged me $20 a visit. The system worked fine for quite a while. But one time, after he cleared our driveway, he returned the next day because some strong winds were causing some drifting. That may have been a problem for some of his other clients. But our driveway was basically wide open, clear of any obstructions like trees on either side, so the wind basically blew the snow across without stopping.

When he returned the next day, I just happened to hear his truck and looked out the window. I was pretty certain he didn't know I was watching; I saw him hit a couple of small drifts at the side of my driveway with his plow and he left. That took him all of about 45 seconds and he was gone. Later, I received a bill for $40 covering two days of plowing.

Obviously, I was not happy. I felt like our agreement was breached, and that he was trying to take advantage of me by charging for the second visit of less than a minute. Rather than call him right away, I decided to take some time to pray and ask God for guidance. This man knew I was a Christian and I felt very strongly in my spirit that I was to make my complaint with a measured response, telling him with simple reason that we had an agreement and I didn't feel good about what he had done.

I would like to tell you that he agreed with me and refunded my $20 for that second visit. But he didn't, and I told him I was sorry that he didn't see things my way and left it at that. I never called on him after that, and we never saw one another again — not because of angst, but simply because we didn't run in the same circles.

Looking back, I am so thankful that I called on help from the Lord before confronting that situation. Because even though I didn't get the result I wanted — I "lost the argument" so to speak — I felt that my Christian witness was more important. And at the very least, I knew that I hadn't put a stumbling block in the way of what God may have wanted to do in that man's life.

A similar situation happened just a couple of years later. I was buying a slightly used wood furnace from someone who went to our church but was a very new believer. We had agreed on a price, but before I was able to pick it up he called me later and said he had seen what they were charging for new furnaces and felt that what we had agreed to was too low. I didn't have a chance to pray about this situation, but I remembered the lesson I had learned from that previous plowing incident. I was quite upset about what I felt was a breach of ethics, but I committed myself to telling the man with a calm, controlled response that I didn't feel good about him breaking our agreement.

To make a long story short, we negotiated a middle-ground price which I thought was still reasonable, even though I strongly disapproved of what he had done. Did I do the right thing? Some would probably have said no. But even though it cost me a little more money, it seemed a small price to pay to keep our relationship intact. As a result, I was able to feed into his spiritual life for quite some time after that. This ended up being the result of obeying the instruction of Jesus in Luke 6:29:

If someone strikes you on the cheek, turn to him the other also. If someone takes your cloak, do not stop him from taking your tunic. Give to everyone who asks you, and if anyone takes what belongs to you, do not demand it back.

A HEALTHY DIET RICH IN FRUIT

I've mentioned the fruit of the Spirit a couple of times now. For those who aren't familiar with this phrase, it is found in Galatians 5:22-23: "But the fruit of the Spirit is love, joy, patience, kindness, goodness, faithfulness, gentleness, self-control. Against such things there is no law."

My late mother was the greatest example of the fruit of the Spirit in my life. When I would do admittedly dumb things — first as a child, then as a teen, and even as an adult — her response regularly was so patient, gentle, and kind. I would say that her loving example as a believer in Jesus was the greatest contributor to my decision as a young boy to make Him my Savior and Lord as well. Who knows how many lives could be touched for the Kingdom if all who call themselves by Jesus' name would reflect the fruit of the Spirit in a similar way to my precious mom?

But you know what? There is a reason it is called the fruit of the *Spirit*. We can't fake it. These attitudes are not inherent to us as humans. We can succeed occasionally in our attempts to be Christlike on our own, but our sinful natures will continue to intrude to the point of discouraging us and damaging our witness for Christ.

That is exactly where I was for many years in my Christian walk. How did that change? I wanted to serve the Lord as a young man, but there were many things that were diverting my attention away from Him. I had issues with anger that started to control me, and it came to a point where my marriage was falling apart and I appeared to be losing everything that I held dear. The thought of not being able to spend each day with my two young daughters was more than I could take.

I could relate very well to Robin Williams' character in the movie *Mrs. Doubtfire* (20th Century Fox, 1993). When his wife sought a divorce and was given custody of their three young kids, he couldn't bear the thought of not being able to be with them every day. So he came up with the idea of applying for the after-school nanny job. But in order to get hired, he had to fool his estranged wife into believing he was someone else. So he dressed up as "Mrs. Doubtfire" so he could still be a part of the everyday lives of his young children.

My approach was a little less dramatic and much less humorous. In that period of deep brokenness I cried out to God and recommitted my life to Him. As soon as I made it a daily practice to study the Bible, pray, and praise Him, my attitudes began to reflect the fruit of the Spirit in increasing measure because I was no longer trying to do it on my own. Soon my wife saw the change in me and reconciliation began.

I had invited the Holy Spirit to have greater control over my life and He accepted the invitation. God taught me this principle in my spirit before I found it in the Bible. But eventually I discovered an example when I read the account of Peter's denial of Jesus in Matthew 26. In verses 31-35, Peter courageously expressed that he would die with Jesus before he would disown him. But later that very night, in verses 69-75, Peter denied knowing Jesus three times. Why? The answer lies in what happened shortly after his firm declaration of loyalty.

Jesus went to a place called Gethsemane to pray and He brought Peter and two other disciples with Him. This was the night before His impending crucifixion. In the midst of His own anguish, Jesus was further sorrowed that Peter and the two other disciples fell asleep. In verse 41 Jesus said to Peter:

"Watch and pray so that you will not fall into temptation. The spirit is willing, but the body is weak."

Jesus knew that Peter wanted to do what was right, but wasn't strong enough in his own small "s" spirit. He also was aware that Peter would need the help of the capital "S" Spirit, the Holy Spirit, to assist him in overcoming the temptation that was to come. Peter's prayers would have been the invitation the Holy Spirit needed to shield him from the darts Satan was about to toss his way. Instead Peter was not clothed in the supernatural armor needed to repel the attack and he fell into sin, denying his relationship with Jesus.

That's the kind of spiritual protection that began to benefit my life once I focused on fully submitting myself to God. People who didn't know me in those days can't believe it when I tell them I once had anger issues because they see the overall peace the Lord has brought to my countenance. And the same can happen for anyone, no matter where they have been or what they have done.

In a remarkable example of this, Bart Millard, lead singer for the popular Christian band Mercy Me, had a very abusive father growing up. When Bart was a teenager his father developed cancer. While the cancer grew in his body he made a choice to accept Jesus as his Savior. Bart said that he was skeptical of his father's conversion at first because of the horrible tyrant he had been. But in the next four years before his father's death, Bart began to realize the man who had brutalized him throughout his childhood was very different. The fruit of the Spirit began to become more and more evident in his father's life.

With deep regret, Bart's dad apologized to him for the way he had treated him and said he wished he could go back and change the past. He became a totally new man to the point where Bart knew that the Spirit of God had amazing power to bring about change in individual lives.

The transformed life experienced by Bart's father literally became a testimony to the rulers of the world. In February 2017, Bart had a chance to share his story with the president, vice president, members of Congress, and several other world leaders at the annual National Prayer Breakfast in Washington D.C. Bart briefly told the assembled crowd about his abusive history with his father. Then he shared how Jesus changed his dad completely from being a "monster" to a man who was "desperately and passionately in love with Jesus."

Bart concluded his thoughts by saying that this miraculous transformation set him on a passion to spread the Gospel — because if Jesus could change his dad, He could change anybody! Ever since, Bart has been singing to the glory of Jesus, including a couple of songs about his father and his desire to see him again in heaven someday.

NOT A TRIVIAL PURSUIT

The transformation in Bart Millard's father was in keeping with what all believers should experience when they accept Jesus as their Savior. Jesus says in Matthew 3:8: "Produce fruit in keeping with repentance." The Greek word for repent, metanoeo, literally means to "turn around." So the decision to make Jesus our *Savior* necessarily means we are to make Him our *Lord* as well. We are to turn around, forsaking our past lives of sin, toward an ongoing life of holiness that honors God. Bart's father certainly did a complete turnabout — a great example for each one of us.

But it has been my sad observation in recent days that many Christians are either not aware, or for some reason aren't acknowledging, that the Holy Spirit has power to bring transformation to their lives. It appears that many of my brothers and sisters in Christ have decided that one of the most noble things we can do is proclaim that we are all chronic, abject spiritual failures that could never possibly obtain any semblance of personal holiness.

Any discussion of the observed, unquestioned sinful behavior of another is often quickly followed up by the uninspiring comment, "Well, we all have our issues." Now certainly this is true. But by openly saying that, aren't we effectively feeding the thought that we should give up on any pursuit of discernible righteousness? After all, as we continually proclaim ourselves to be hopelessly wretched creatures, we are essentially looking at disobedience to God as inevitable.

This very issue surfaced recently when I was having a discussion with a small group of Christians. It was mentioned that a well-known singer who had claimed to be a follower of Jesus for many years occasionally said a very obscene swear word. Despite this, one of those in the discussion said, "I have no doubt that he really is a Christian." I was shocked! I made no secret of the fact that I questioned this singer's spiritual disposition if, after several decades as a self-proclaimed brother in Christ, he was still commonly using the most vulgar of profanities.

By the way, the Bible tells us that even though we can't judge a person's heart, it is appropriate to make judgments based on their evident fruit. Paul wrote in Galatians 6:1: "Brothers, if someone is caught in a sin, you who are spiritual should restore him gently. But watch yourself, or you also may be tempted." (I'll share more on proper and improper biblical judgment in chapter 9.)

After expressing my thoughts, one of the others in the discussion made the aforementioned comment in a distinctly matter-of-fact way, "Well, we all have issues." But I will ask the question again. Does this give us permission to not even try to achieve righteousness?

In his fantastic book *The Pursuit of Holiness*, Jerry Bridges wrote:

"It is time for us Christians to face up to our responsibility for holiness. Too often we say we are 'defeated'
by this or that sin. No, we are not defeated; we are
simply disobedient!...When I say I am defeated by
some sin, I am unconsciously slipping out from under
my responsibility...We need to brace ourselves up and
to realize that we are responsible for our thoughts, attitudes, and actions."[8]

Can you imagine our earthly parents giving us instructions
to do the dishes, or mow the lawn, or clean our rooms, and
then saying, "but you're such a lowly, out-of-control individual that you might as well not even try. In fact, I know
you won't be able to succeed so I won't hold you accountable
when you do fall short." That's just not going to happen. And
it's no different with our heavenly parent, Father God.

Once we become Christians, the Bible tells us over and
over again that we are supposed to become "new creations."
Ephesians 4:22-24 says:

You were taught, with regard to your former way of
life, to put off your old self, which is being corrupted
by its deceitful desires; to be made new in the attitude
of your minds; and to put on the new self, created to
be like God in true righteousness and holiness."

These verses apply to every aspect of being a believer in
Jesus. And if I could once again ask you to consider the singer
we discussed a few moments ago, in verse 29 of that same
passage it says: "Do not let any unwholesome talk come out
of your mouths..." It would be hard to win the argument if you
claim that his use of the most profane of all obscene words is
not "unwholesome talk."

But to me, this singer's common use of such a vile word
after declaring a long-term allegiance to Christ wasn't the
most troubling part of the conversation. More disturbing was

the fact that some of the brothers and sisters who were joining me in the discussion seemed to have the attitude that there was very little wrong with this obvious contradiction, declaring only that "we all have our issues."

To be sure, if we continually tell ourselves that we are spiritually untamable and can't possibly live up to anything but the most remedial level of righteousness, then we will fulfill that expectation every time. There needs to be a paradigm shift back to the biblical understanding that the pursuit of holiness is a mandatory responsibility, and largely attainable through the power of the Holy Spirit working in our lives.

Here are just a few of the verses that support this assessment:

- Proverbs 15:9 — "The Lord detests the way of the wicked but he loves those who pursue righteousness."

- 1 Timothy 6:11 — "But you, man of God, flee from all this, and pursue righteousness, godliness, faith, love, endurance and gentleness."

- 2 Timothy 2:22 — "Flee the evil desires of youth, and pursue righteousness, faith, love and peace, along with those who call on the Lord out of a pure heart."

- 1 Peter 3:11-12 — "For the eyes of the Lord are on the righteous and his ears are attentive to their prayer, but the face of the Lord is against those who do evil."

Clearly the pursuit of righteousness and holiness is not optional in the eyes of God. And it should be just as obvious that He wouldn't give us these commands time and time again if it was a hopeless quest. By the way, look at that last passage again from 1 Peter. When our committed pursuit inevitably results in a level of success, what a great reward awaits. The eyes of the Lord are upon us, and He is attentive to our prayers!

CONCLUDING THOUGHT

Philippians 2:3-4 affirms that in the eyes of God a Christlike, Spirit-controlled attitude is not optional for the believer in Jesus:

Do nothing out of selfish ambition or vain conceit, but in humility consider others better than yourselves. Each of you should look not only to your own interests, but also the interests of others.

If we have an attitude of humility with a focus on the good of others — especially the eternal good — we will treat them in ways that will be noticed and can really make a difference in their lives.

When we respond to people in ways that reflect the fruit of the Spirit, that is when our light truly shines for Jesus. This is one of the most important messages I want to convey in these pages. Because unless we are godly in our attitudes, we have not earned the right to be heard — either by fellow believers whom we are trying to mentor, or by those who are not yet Christians. But if we have a reliably Christlike countenance we will provide the Holy Spirit with significant opportunities to touch lives for the Kingdom. People will be much more open to what we have to say. Otherwise, they will likely be repelled by our apparent hypocrisy.

7-ACTIONS: PIERCING THE DARKNESS

The fact of the matter is, very few non-Christians are willing to show us grace when we fall short of what we should be. They often use these perceived instances of hypocrisy as their reason to reject Christ. So every effort should be made to prioritize our spiritual growth.

As the Holy Spirit transforms us on the inside through our attitudes, it should then become evident on the outside through the actions and activities that are a part of our lives. These attributes should be related. As I've discussed previously, if we try to please the Lord by legalistically keeping man-made rules regarding certain actions and activities, but our attitudes are not in keeping with the fruit of the Spirit, then we can end up doing more harm than good for the cause of Christ. Conversely, if our attitudes reflect the fruit of the Spirit, but are not evident in our actions and activities, then we can also end up being a detriment to the Kingdom. As James 2:17-18 says:

> In the same way, faith by itself, if it is not accompanied by action, is dead. But someone will say, "You have faith; I have deeds." Show me your faith without deeds, and I will show you my faith by what I do.

One time I was talking with a woman who disagreed with my assessment that the most effective Christian witness includes righteousness in all of these areas — attitudes, actions, and activities. I'll call her Peggy. Peggy used her marriage as an analogy. She mentioned that it didn't matter so much to her what her husband did for her, but rather, that her husband loved her from the heart. It was Peggy's way of saying that God doesn't care that much about how we live our lives as long as He knows we truly love Him. So in her mind having the right attitude as a Christian took center stage, while actions and activities weren't really all that important.

I decided to take Peggy's analogy in a different direction to prove *my* point. I suggested that her husband could do wonderful things like shower her with gifts, take her out on regular dates, and praise her with uplifting words. But that would be meaningless if he did these things while at the same time was being unfaithful to her with other women. This would be like the person who thinks that being righteous in our actions and activities is all that matters, but an attitude of faithfulness to God is not important. (Once again this brings to mind those white-washed tombs, the Pharisees.) What Jesus said in Matthew 7:22-23 tells us of the inadequacy of such a works-only based theology:

> "Many will say to me on that day, 'Lord, Lord, did we not prophesy in your name, and in your name drive out demons and perform many miracles?' Then I will tell them plainly, 'I never knew you. Away from me you evil-doers!'"

These are very strong words from Jesus Himself. Clearly there cannot be a disconnect between what we have *within* as Christians and those things that are a part of our lives *without*. In other words, what people see of us on the outside should reflect the love we have for the Lord on the inside, and vice versa. I believe this to be critically important in upholding the reputation of the Christ we represent.

THE IMPORTANCE OF TOTAL COMMITMENT

I'd like to specifically look at football again for just a minute. (You'll have to forgive me, but sports create so many great analogies!) Let's say two men are invited to become part of the best football team in the league. They both accept the invitation. It is clear that the other players are more familiar with the playbook and are physically built up, far beyond the present condition of these two new recruits.

So one of them attends the practices, eager to learn and grow as a player. He begins the process of learning the playbook, spending time with his new teammates to learn the ins and outs of the game, building himself up physically, and basically doing whatever he can to become a valuable part of the team. He understands that the team name on the front of the uniform is more important than the name of the individual on the back. He knows that if he is not prepared when the opportunity comes to help the team, he may be more of a detriment than an asset. It is clear that his ambitions are not selfish; it is in his heart to devote himself fully to the good of the team. When he finally gets a chance to play, his preparation pays off as he comes through and helps the team win another game.

The other recruit, after accepting the invitation to join, is happy to proclaim his association with the team. But he attends the practices only because he is supposed to. The time he spends with his teammates is more about having fun than about learning the game and becoming a better player. He rarely spends time in the playbook or in the exercise room. So when the time comes and the coach tells him to enter the game, he is not prepared. He is simply not ready for the challenge before him and he fails, and the team loses as a result. The question has to be asked, did he really join the team in his heart? Or did he claim association with the team for selfish reasons?

The analogy here is hopefully pretty obvious. Put it in terms of the two men accepting Christ as their Savior. The first man dutifully reads the Bible and goes to church so he can learn and grow. So when the opportunities are presented, the preparation pays off. He becomes an effective asset to the "team," consistently representing his Christian faith well and winning victories for the Kingdom.

The second man, after proclaiming faith in Christ, goes to church only occasionally — maybe on potluck Sundays or during other events of good fellowship. He rarely reads his Bible or does anything else to help him grow in his faith. So when he has a chance to stand up for Christ he falls short more often than not, damaging the reputation of the One he claims to represent and losing potential souls for the Kingdom.

The first man is clearly the one who God can use, because he has committed himself to putting action behind his godly attitude. Now you may be saying, "Hey, cut that second man some slack. Nobody's perfect!" And this is very true. But the fact of the matter is, very few non-Christians are willing to show us grace when we fall short of what we should be. They often use these perceived instances of hypocrisy as their reason to reject Christ. So every effort should be made to prioritize our spiritual growth.

I know that God has cut *me* some slack, forgiving me for those times when I have not lived up to what I should have been as His servant. But I grieve the thought that I have hurt people, many of whom knew I was a Christian. It is so painful to believe that in my ignorance and immaturity I may have been responsible for turning people away from the God I love. I pray virtually every day that God will mend any lingering damage I potentially brought to them or the reputation of Christ.

GROWING UP IS NOT OPTIONAL

This leads to the point of what I am trying to say. Especially for new believers there will be a period where they will still have some rough edges for God to smooth out in their attitudes and actions, as well as the activities they choose to participate in. But because the stakes are so high — eternity is in the balance — it would behoove them to make growing up in their faith a top priority.

I had a friend who had a wonderful, childlike sense of humor. When he was around 50 years old, he would often say, "Growing old is mandatory; growing up is optional!" This may be true, and even acceptable, when it comes to living life with an endearing personality. But it is entirely unacceptable, and even tragic, to have that belief in a spiritual sense.

The song "The Motions" by Matthew West (2009, Sparrow Records) has some fantastic lyrics that address the urgency of growing up in our faith in order to be an asset to the Kingdom rather than a hindrance:

> I don't wanna go through the motions
> I don't wanna go one more day
> Without Your all-consuming passion inside of me
> I don't wanna spend my whole life asking,
> "What if I had given everything,
> Instead of going through the motions?"

I would give anything if I could go back and relate to my family, friends, co-workers — really everyone who has been a part of my life — with a greater level of spiritual maturity right from my very earliest days as a Christian. Everyone who has been a believer even just a very short time should already be making an effort to grow in their faith, instead of "going through the motions."

Consider the newborn baby. Not a lot is expected of them, and justifiably so. However, there would be concern if an otherwise healthy child was still wearing diapers and eating baby food at the age of five. And while it can be aggravating that a toddler wants to get into anything and everything around the house, this is really a very healthy sign. Their precious little minds are wanting to absorb all the knowledge they can about what is around them.

Similarly, "baby" Christians need time to develop in their faith. But sadly, some who become born again believers in Jesus seem too content to remain infants. If they do not have a sincere desire to absorb all the knowledge they can as part of their new life in Christ, then there is cause for concern about their spiritual health. In Hebrews 5:12-6:1 the writer, inspired by the Holy Spirit, scolds those who have not made an attempt to mature in their faith:

> You need milk, not solid food! Anyone who lives on milk, being still an infant, is not acquainted with the teaching about righteousness. But solid food is for the mature, who by constant use have trained themselves to distinguish good from evil. Therefore let us leave the elementary teachings about Christ and go on to maturity...

Unfortunately, this type of spiritual immaturity in some believers can go on for years, with the resultant behaviors bringing damage to the reputation of our Lord.

Even in the Christian ministries I have been a part of, some of my fellow employees apparently believed they were exempt from having to display the fruit of the Spirit when interacting with co-workers. Somehow in their minds the love, joy, peace, patience, kindness, goodness, faithfulness, gentleness, and self-control spoken of in Galatians 5:22-23 didn't apply when at the workplace. I have also been in the presence of a pastor and ministry leader or two when they were exhibiting shamefully harsh, judgmental, and arrogant behavior. I can remember thinking more than once that if I was not fully convinced of the reality of the Gospel I would never want to become a Christian because of their examples.

I am like so many others. I have been hurt badly at times by immature believers. To my shame, as a "baby" who grew up too slowly, I have been among those who occasionally have caused the hurt. And that is why I encourage each of you who claim the name of Christ to explore and absorb all you can of His Kingdom and His righteousness. Invite the Holy Spirit to take control of your life as quickly and completely as possible so He can mold you into a good and faithful servant who consistently brings glory to the Lord. This will have the effect of drawing people to Him, rather than repelling them.

Each Christian is a work in progress. We can't live assuming that once we express faith in Jesus we can stay the way we are. No, God loves us too much for that. He will continue day by day, as we submit ourselves to Him, making us into Kingdom warriors who can effectively win the spiritual battles that advance His purposes.

One thing I'd like to point out is that we will never arrive at a place of spiritual perfection while on this earth. Even mature believers need to be consistently on guard. I personally can testify to that fact. Despite a significant level of accrued biblical knowledge, and an all-encompassing desire to honor God, I have been guilty more than once in recent years of poor judgment driven by feelings over godly reason.

In particular, we as Christians have to be so careful not to make choices and decisions which are prompted by pain or fear. Satan is the author of pain and fear and he often uses these things to cloud our discernment. He is very crafty, subtly tempting us into sin which has the potential to be very destructive to our witness for Jesus. At times such as these, it is wise to heed the advice and warnings of other brothers and sisters in Christ who are viewing the situation from a less emotion driven perspective.

As you become more committed in your devotion to God, and consequently more effective in your service to Him, you can expect increased attacks from the powers of darkness. Satan will not like the disruption you are bringing to his evil plans and he will do whatever he can to destroy your witness for Christ. Make sure to keep your spiritual armor on (Ephesians 6:10-18), spending time with God daily in His Word and in prayer, so you can repel the enemy's advances.

If you do fall, don't let Satan overwhelm you with condemnation. Just sincerely repent, put the past failure behind you, and commit to doing better from that moment on. As you desire to serve God, you need to remember that His grace is sufficient to cover all sins and He forgives the truly humble, repentant heart. And that is the type of heart God can continually use to advance His purposes going forward.

LIVING AS SHEEP

One of the important ways God works through us is spelled out in the parable of the sheep and goats in Matthew 25:31-46. In this passage, the sheep (representing Christians) who feed the hungry, give water to the thirsty, take in needy strangers, clothe those who need clothing, look after the sick, and visit those in prison are among those who go to heaven. Similarly in James 1:27 it says: "Religion that God our Father accepts as pure and faultless is this: to look after orphans and widows in their distress and to keep oneself from being polluted by the world."

It's important to note that in the first century when this was written there were no established government programs to take care of children or women who had lost their fathers and husbands. So they were among the most vulnerable people in the culture. That is why orphans and widows were specifically mentioned in this passage. God considers caring for the helpless, weak, and powerless to be the most tangible way we as Christians can express honor to Him through our actions.

However, we must keep in mind that if these acts of compassion are done as a way of trying to gain favor with God, or to make a name for ourselves, then it is an example of "being polluted by the world." But if these actions reflect a love for people that truly grows out of a genuine love for Christ in our hearts, then they are among the most pure and faultless ways we can express our faith.

In relation to this subject, I'd like to mention a friend of mine who has a heart as deep as the ocean for the orphans who need someone to permanently love and care for them. He consistently points out the large number of foster children who need a loving family they can call their own. As Christians, there are few more pure and faultless ways to express our faith than to take such children into our homes.

I know that not all people have the ability to become foster or adoptive parents. But if it is possible, think of the impact you could have on these kids! I have a dear pastor friend and his wife who have fostered many children over the years, and they have adopted several of them. When the pastor told me about this, I expressed my amazement at their commitment. He said they looked at it as a form of evangelism — lovingly caring for the *temporal* needs of these kids with an eye on their *eternal* needs, nurturing them toward faith in Jesus Christ. When you think about it, foster and adoptive parenting provides a tremendous opportunity to be a conduit of God's love to those who have often suffered much in their young lives.

There is one other thing I'd like to mention briefly as a way of clarification. It is not my intention to get political in this book, but I do think it's important to point out that God did not instruct governments to provide for all of the needs mentioned in Matthew 25, nor did he instruct anyone to take anything from anybody else against their will to provide for these types of needs. These were instructions God gave to His people to voluntarily give of themselves as a way of honoring Him and helping others. And once again, when we are obedient in this it opens up opportunities for the Holy Spirit to go to work in the lives of those we are serving.

As an example, in 2004 a horrific tsunami struck the Indian Ocean. When the waters reached land, more than 200,000 people were killed in 14 different countries. The worst hit were Indonesia, Sri Lanka, India, and Thailand. In terms of religion, at that time Indonesia was about 87 percent Muslim, Sri Lanka 70 percent Buddhist, India 80 percent Hindu, and Thailand 95 percent Buddhist. Before the tsunami, these nations allowed little or no freedom of religion. In the aftermath, because of the tremendous devastation, Christian organizations were allowed in to do relief work.

To make a long story short, this expression of compassion to those who in many cases had been previously hostile to Christianity led to thousands of people coming to faith in Jesus in the ensuing months. God had allowed a short-term tragedy to bring about glorious eternal results for countless individuals. I believe that is why putting our faith into action in such compassionate ways is so important to God.

If we can't give hands on help, there is also the option of giving financially. There are so many ministries that are worthy of support. An example would be pregnancy resource centers. They provide love and assistance to mothers and fathers experiencing unplanned pregnancies, both before and after a birth, as a way of encouraging them to choose life for their unborn child. As a result, many of these women and men accept Jesus as their Savior and are born again, while their babies are born for the first time.

Whatever ministry you may consider supporting, I would encourage you to do a little homework to make sure they are completely biblical in their beliefs. Some organizations can seem legitimate, but are really not as they appear. As an example, there is an organization with a very positive sounding name — The Military Religious Freedom Foundation — but their intentional focus is actually on diminishing the influence of Christianity in the military.

TAMING THE TONGUE

The final issue I would like to address in this chapter has to do with the way we use our tongues. In recent years, the casualness that I have discussed previously seems to have infected the Kingdom of God in the words we use and the type of things we talk about.

James 3 is the consummate chapter relating to the tongue; how important it is to speak appropriately, and how difficult that can be. In verse 8 James writes that "no man can tame the tongue." That's why I believe the only initial evidence we find in the Bible for the baptism in the Holy Spirit is speaking in an unknown language. Because if the Holy Spirit controls the tongue to the point that we can speak a language we have never learned, then He has clearly been put in charge of a submitted life. (We'll discuss this in more detail in chapters 12 and 13.)

It is just like a bit in the mouth of a horse in verse 3, or the rudder on a ship in verse 4. Those small pieces can control the direction of the much larger whole. When the Holy Spirit is in control of the tongue, He has also been put into a position to control the direction of the whole person. Verse 9 says: "With the tongue we praise our Lord and Father, and with it we curse men, who have been made in God's likeness."

We should never underestimate how important it is to use our tongues in ways that glorify the Lord. In recent days there have been certain evangelists and pastors of questionable credibility who have begun the practice of using occasional profanity. In some cases, it is used as a way of shocking their audiences into getting the point of their messages. For others it is being used as a way of reaching out to the unsaved; a clearly misguided attempt to be all things to all people as Paul talked about in 1 Corinthians 9:19-23.

But I learned firsthand during my eight years working at a sheriff's office that using profane words can dim the witness of a Christian. It was well-known among my co-workers that I was a follower of Jesus, and apparently the tragic human drama that law enforcement officers deal with regularly had taken a spiritual toll on other believers before me. Because one deputy, I'll call him Ken, told me that after a while the righteousness of every self-proclaimed Christian who came through there eventually diminished. He was certain the same thing would happen to me.

One day several months later, I was sharing a story with a different deputy when I quoted a swear word spoken by another person. Ken happened to overhear me and quickly said, "Did you just swear? See, I knew that Christian stuff wouldn't last!" All I did was quote somebody else saying one word of profanity, and my commitment to Jesus came into question.

This incident was verifiable proof to me that the words we use really do matter as we live out our faith. Ken needed to see somebody who gave him reason to believe that Christianity was more than just a nonsensical and worthless religion, and my words had the ability to negate any credibility I had as a believer in his eyes. Needless to say, from that moment on I made it a practice never to even quote somebody else saying a swear word. In two verses in Ephesians, 4:29 and 5:4, Paul puts the matter into context:

> Do not let any unwholesome talk come out of your mouths, but only what is helpful for building others up according to their needs, that it may benefit those who listen...Nor should there be obscenity, foolish talk or coarse joking, which are out of place, but rather thanksgiving.

Of course, these verses apply to more than just cursing. We should never tell or laugh at dirty jokes. We shouldn't make any mean-spirited degrading or belittling comments in our conversations with others. (After growing up with two brothers, this is one thing the Lord is still working out of me!) And as men we shouldn't be participants in making inappropriate comments to one another about those captivating women who cross our paths.

Finally, gossip is an issue that should not be overlooked when discussing the proper use of the tongue. The book of Proverbs says gossip betrays a confidence (11:13, 20:19) and can separate close friends (16:28). It also works to fuel quarrels (26:20). It causes broken trusts and hurt feelings. When a Christian is guilty of gossip it can repel people from the very Gospel we want them to embrace.

This is a very easy sin to fall into, even for the mature believer. But there is one thing that has helped me significantly when the temptation comes to gossip against another. I try to talk with the mindset that the person who is the focus of the discussion is actually in the room. It is amazing how that can aid in keeping a conversation God-honoring. (And it can prevent embarrassment and hurt feelings should that person just happen to, say, come around the corner and overhear what is being said.)

These are just a few examples of unwholesome and foolish talk that are completely out of place for Christians. Instead, we should speak words that are uplifting, beneficial, and full of thankfulness. This will be useful in drawing people to us, and they will be far more open to what we have to say about the One who makes us that way.

CONCLUDING THOUGHT

We must never forget what we're supposed to look like as Christians. We should read the Word of God daily and do what it says. When we are in doubt about what pleases God, we should spend time in prayer and seek his guidance. And we should respond to the conviction of the Holy Spirit.

As you continue to seek after God, and you begin to feel uneasy about certain aspects of how you are living your life, then understand it is likely the Holy Spirit at work prompting you toward greater sanctification. That's when you begin to look more like Jesus and can have a more powerful and effective ministry than you may have ever dreamed possible.

I love a line in the 2005 Hallmark Channel movie *Love's Long Journey,* based on the book of the same name by Janette Oke.[9] A hired hand on a nineteenth century farm said to others laboring with him that he was planning on going to church the next Sunday with the godly young couple they were working for.

When these tough-as-nails men asked him why he said, "If believin' the way they does, makes them the way they is, then it bears lookin' into." Oh that the world would say that about each one of us as they clearly see the evidence of God's love and righteousness in our daily lives!

8–ACTIONS: CREATING A WONDERFUL LIGHT

God only wants us to do our best to honor Him in every area of our lives. And when we make the intentional choice to do that, even when we inevitably fall short of perfection, God can still work through us to bring victories for His Kingdom.

P rofessional athletes have a preseason before the regular season starts to allow them time to get into "game shape." They are far more mistake prone until they knock off the rust from the off-season. For new players, it provides an opportunity to learn the playbook and find out if they have what it takes to make the roster. This all takes place when the outcome is not as important because the preseason games don't count in the standings.

Spiritually speaking, we don't have the convenience of getting into game shape during a time when the stakes are not so high. When we accept Jesus as our Savior and Lord, and God begins His good work in us, it is already the "regular season." So while we are learning from our playbook, the Bible, the mistakes we make — even as the newest of believers — are noticed by others and the ramifications can be damaging to the "team."

In 1 Timothy 3:7, Paul says that a spiritual leader "...must also have a good reputation with outsiders, so that he will not fall into disgrace and into the devil's trap." And this really applies to each believer in Jesus, no matter where we are in our Christian walk. If we bring damage to our own reputation by our ungodly actions, that has the residual effect of damaging the reputation of the Lord we are supposed to represent. It's a trap of the devil that hinders our witness and makes it ineffective.

The late Brennan Manning, who passed away in 2013, was a former priest, public speaker, and author who was probably best known for his book *The Ragamuffin Gospel*.[10] He said, "The greatest single cause of atheism in the world today is Christians who acknowledge Jesus with their lips then walk out the door and deny him by their lifestyle. That is what an unbelieving world simply finds unbelievable."

I agree wholeheartedly with Manning's assessment. And that is why our efforts toward sanctification — studying our Bibles and praying daily, going to church regularly, and taking advantage of other spiritual growth opportunities — are important right from the start and must never end no matter how mature we become in our faith.

Of course, none of us will ever be perfect and sin free in this life. As 1 John 1:8 says: "If we claim to be without sin, we deceive ourselves and the truth is not in us." However, we must not use this fact as an excuse to quit trying either. We *should not* allow Satan to overwhelm us with condemnation when we fall, but we *should* respond positively to the conviction of the Holy Spirit by picking ourselves up and resolving to do better the next time with His help.

WHEN LIGHT PIERCES THE DARKNESS

In North Korea, one of the most atheistic and cruel nations on the earth, the children are brainwashed into believing that Christians are evil people. A 26-year-old North Korean woman named Jo shared her testimony in the March 22nd, 2014 edition of *World* magazine. She said that as a little girl she, her mother, and sister — gripped by hunger — slipped out of North Korea and into China in search of food. That night, Jo was on a road when she heard music coming from a home. She listened for a while and began to cry. A woman inside the residence heard Jo and invited her in to what turned out to be a house church.

Over the next several months Jo would sneak out of her home from time to time, cross into China, and visit this small church. When her mother found out, she warned Jo about the perceived cruelty of Christians. But God's love had been revealed to Jo through the lives of these believers. It was the consistent, Christlike actions of these people that convinced Jo of the truth of the Gospel and she became a Christian. The Chinese authorities later captured Jo, her mother, and sister after they again illegally crossed the border in an attempt to find food. They were returned to North Korea where they suffered brutal treatment at the hands of prison guards.

Jo credits prayer for their eventual release. She had shared her new-found faith with her mother and sister, and today these women are in the United States and are all Christians; three more souls saved for eternity because of believers in a Chinese house church whose outward lives reflected the faith they had within.

I have also seen personally how a love for Christ expressed through a righteous life can have a very positive impact on the Kingdom. In Matthew 5:14-16 Jesus says:

> "You are the light of the world. A city on a hill cannot be hidden. Neither do people light a lamp and put it under a bowl. Instead they put it on its stand, and it gives light to everyone in the house. In the same way, let your light shine before men, that they may see your good deeds and praise your Father in heaven."

In my teen years I was of the rather naive belief that all of the kids in my church youth group were pretty much like me — falling short once in a while but certainly doing their best to live for the Lord. I was very surprised when I began a job at a company owned by one of our church members. On my first day, several of my new co-workers were smoking cigarettes in the break room. One of them was a friend from my church youth group, who I'll call Nate. I realized even then that smoking cigarettes didn't mean my friend was necessarily a horribly corrupt pagan. But I was still shocked. And as I began to learn more about Nate, it was clear the cigarettes were just one indicator of a life that had turned to rebellion against God.

It wasn't long before I became aware that there were others in my youth group who were also living a double life. When this small, rebellious faction found out that I knew about Nate but didn't tell parents or pastors, they felt safe to be themselves around me — which included doing drugs and alcohol. Despite their lifestyle, I enjoyed being with them. They were good to me and made me feel important, which meant so much to me as a typical teenager. Even though I was with them at certain times when these things were going on, I didn't condone or participate in it; I just wanted to be a part of this group where I felt so accepted.

There came a point after several months of this that the Holy Spirit appeared to be convicting Nate of the way he was living. He made an attempt to recommit his life to the Lord, and he talked to our youth pastor about what had been going on in his life. I wasn't aware of this until later, but Nate had gone to him expressing a desire to change. The youth pastor shared with me that Nate had said he wanted to get those destructive things out of his life. He told me that Nate had said with conviction, "If Randy can do it, I can do it."

Obviously, I was pleasantly delighted to hear this! I had no idea that my desire to honor the Lord with my actions was actually being seen. In fact, I felt I should have been doing more to be a better witness for Him. But clearly the Holy Spirit was able to use my commitment, as immature and imperfect as it was, to His glory.

I had another friend in those days who I met in our neighborhood. I'll call him Matt. I'm not exactly sure how Matt and I became friends. We ran in different circles, but became very close before I went off to Bible college. He hung with two groups of friends; the relatively tame group of guys that I was associated with, and some guys who were into doing drugs and alcohol among other things. As I recall, Matt said his parents were Christians, but the legalistic type like we've discussed previously where there were a lot of rules but very little love in the home. His response was to rebel and do pretty much everything his parents would not have wanted him to do.

As we grew closer as friends, I slowly began to see a change in Matt. Just like with Nate, Matt and I had a lot of fun together but I wouldn't participate in the destructive behaviors that were a part of his life at the time. Somewhere along the line, God began to get through to Matt. I remember one night when he made a tangible commitment in front of me to change his ways. Matt took a bag of marijuana and simply dumped it in the grass. He said the pot was worth hundreds of dollars, and that if his other friends knew what he had just done they would have beaten him to a pulp. But he didn't care. This ended up being another example of where my outward actions reflected my inward attitude of commitment to Jesus, and the results made an impact for the Kingdom.

Now please don't misinterpret this as me somehow patting myself on the back here. After these very positive events I had some years, as I've mentioned, where I am ashamed of the example I was for Christ. But praise the Lord, by His matchless grace, He is willing to forgive a repentant heart. And as I've grown older, I continue to see the principle burst into reality that a life committed to righteousness before God and man is a life that He can use for His glory.

As A.W. Tozer wrote in his classic book, *The Pursuit of God*:

The man of God set his heart to exalt God above all;
God accepted his intention as fact and acted accordingly.
Not perfection, but holy intention made the difference.[11]

Put another way, God only wants us to do our best to honor Him in every area of our lives. And when we make the intentional choice to do that, even when we inevitably fall short of perfection, God can still work through us to bring victories for His Kingdom.

WHEN DARKNESS DIMS THE LIGHT

Unfortunately, the opposite is true as well. When our actions don't match our proclaimed commitment to Jesus, it can repel the very people we are trying to reach.

Many athletes who say they are Christians provide a good case in point. I have seen self-proclaimed believers do things on camera during games that have made me cringe, including self-aggrandizing celebrations, cursing that took little expertise in the art of lip-reading to understand, and embarrassing verbal or physical confrontations that were prompted by uncontrolled anger. There have even been several athletes that I actually disliked because of their regular displays of pride and arrogance, only to find out later that they were self-proclaimed Christians. Does this reflect well on the One we are supposed to be glorifying with our lives?

Retired NFL defensive end Jared Allen is among those pro athletes who believed in Jesus for many years, but his actions and language were not bringing glory to the Lord. That changed in 2011, however, when he was a member of the Minnesota Vikings.

In an interview the following year on the Christian Broadcasting Network, Allen said that he had been confronted with a sobering question during a chapel service. The team chaplain asked, "If you were arrested for being a Christian today, would there be enough evidence to convict you?" Allen honestly answered "No." He said in the interview: "People will tell you that believing in Jesus is the most important thing, which it is. But let's be honest, you gotta walk the walk." And that's what he began doing from that moment on.

Yes, belief in Jesus and His sacrifice on the cross is what matters for our salvation. Paul writes in the well-known passage from Ephesians 2:8-9: "For it is by grace you have been saved, through faith–and this not from yourselves, it is the gift of God–not by works so that no one can boast."

But the lesser-known and less-quoted verse that follows is what Allen came to realize in that chapel meeting. Ephesians 2:10 says: "For we are God's workmanship, created in Christ Jesus to do good works, which God prepared in advance for us to do."

Sadly, an overemphasis on the faith aspect of this passage among Christian leadership in recent years is now being seen in the actions of many young believers. As kids have heard time and time again during their formative years that faith is all that matters, and living lives of consecration to God isn't really all that important, they have definitely gotten the message and have been taking it to heart. The residual effect has been an upcoming generation of believers that is largely indifferent in their service to God. Of course there are wonderful exceptions, and praise the Lord for those young people who have chosen to commit their lives passionately and completely to the Lord!

When we are followers of Jesus, it truly *does* matter how we live our lives. You see, we are made right with God by what we do, not by faith alone.

Now, perhaps you just read that last sentence and said I've gone too far. In fact, if I were to say those words in the presence of some believers today I might get soundly criticized for endorsing a works-based theology. But you know what? That sentence is actually straight out of the Bible, from James 2:24

111

(NLT): "So you see, we are made right with God by what we do, not by faith alone." And I assure you, I have not taken this passage out of context.

The point I'm trying to make is that it is indeed correct to say our works, or actions, do not save us. But we do have a responsibility to respond to God's magnificent saving grace by consecrating our lives to him.

PREVENTING STAINS WITHIN THE STAINED-GLASS WINDOWS

Another way that Satan tries to dim the witness of believers is by bringing contention between them. We must remember that the manner in which we treat our brothers and sisters in Christ is of great importance, in the eyes of God and in the eyes of the world. When there is disunity and conflict in a church, it goes a long way toward telling unbelievers that Christianity is not worth their consideration.

It is so sad to hear of churches that have been decimated by individuals who by their unrighteous actions exerted their will and caused hurt to the pastor or other members of their congregations. This has helped contribute to the number of pastors who are leaving the ministry at an alarming rate today, much to the devil's delight. (We need to be praying for our pastors every day as they and their families are prime targets for Satan's attacks.)

But the opposite can be true as well. Jesus says in John 13:35: "By this all men will know you are my disciples, if you love one another."

I know a man I'll call Jason who provided a great example to me of how a serious disagreement in a church should be handled. Jason was one of three board members at his church. There came a time when the pastor wanted to change the requirements for church membership in the bylaws (relating in large part to many of the gray areas discussed in this book).

The pastor characterized it as "showing more grace." Jason looked at it as lowering the standards, allowing a declining society to dictate what would be deemed as acceptable behavior for a church member.

The other two board members sided with the pastor in the dispute. While these board members were fairly young in their walks with Christ, Jason and the pastor were both long-time believers. Jason knew that the way this situation was handled would have implications beyond the importance of well-written bylaws. He understood that the example he and the pastor gave to the other board members and the rest of the church could either glorify the Lord or blow the church apart.

After several months of well-intentioned give and take, trying to work out any type of compromise that could be palatable to both sides, it was decided that two options on each of the disputed portions of the bylaws would be presented to the church members for a vote. When the ballots were counted, the vote favored Jason's position right down the line which obviously disappointed the pastor and the other board members. But rather than glorying in his victory, Jason and his wife prayerfully chose to leave the church to prevent any further disunity.

One of Jason's biggest fears from the start was that the dispute would lead to a church split. He did not want in any way to be responsible for such a thing. So before he left Jason explained to the congregation during a meeting of the members, with the pastor and board members present, his reason for leaving. He felt that if everything was brought out in the open Satan would have no opportunity to wreak havoc in the church once he was gone. Jason admitted that he didn't know for sure if he was right in all he had done. He asked for their forgiveness if he was wrong, but said he did what he believed was right in the eyes of God.

Jason's choice to act in ways that glorified the Lord throughout this difficult dispute ultimately proved to be wise.

There was no church split. And while there were some uncomfortable moments between Jason, the pastor, and the other board members early on, as time passed it became clear in their relationships that all was forgiven. Most importantly, the purposeful actions that were intended to reflect well on God's Kingdom served to maintain relationships and protect the reputation of Christ.

As an aside, there are those who say we shouldn't have membership requirements in our church bylaws; that the Bible should be the lone manual for how we should live our lives as believers. But the Bible is several hundred pages long while bylaws are generally just a few. I contend that bylaws can allow new believers to quickly get an understanding of those behaviors considered by church leadership to be of spiritual concern, and then they can more fully explore the subject later in the Bible. Besides, we have no problem with membership requirements when it comes to various earthly clubs or organizations. Why should we take issue with something as eternally important as establishing expectations for how church members should conduct their lives and represent Christ?

A PROBLEM OF THE AGES

It is so sad when contention arises in a church because of trivial things like the color of the carpet, or the type of seating used in the sanctuary — or even about somewhat more important things like the style of music played during worship. This last issue has caused a great deal of angst in many churches in recent years. This too needs to be handled with the thought of glorifying God first and foremost in our minds. Our second thought, however, should be showing honor and respect to all age groups involved.

Older congregants need to acknowledge that young people have a lot of choices about where to go to church; or if they want to go to church at all. There is nothing wrong with vibrant worship music that appeals to the younger generation. I like what I heard from an elderly gentleman recently. He said he was troubled by the "rockier" worship music after a new, younger pastor took over his church. But he said he looked around and saw young people all over the sanctuary with their eyes closed and hands raised in worship. He then realized the music was being used as a spiritual tool, leading youth in unashamed praise unto the Lord.

Conversely, younger generations need to have a sincere respect for the older people in the church. These are the people who in many cases have invested enormous amounts of time and money over the years to give the church a strong ministry foundation. This legacy should not only be respected, but honored.

For instance, it is a good thing to keep the volume of the worship music at a reasonable level. After all, our ears are a part of our bodies — the temple of the Holy Spirit. So in this way, not only would a moderate volume be showing honor to the older people in the congregation, but would also be expressing thankfulness to the Lord for giving us the blessing of good hearing. (I had a friend who said I sounded like an old "fuddy-duddy" for making such a comment. Interestingly, he was wearing his much-needed hearing aids when he said that. That's an argument won for Randy!) And I would submit that any instrument that is too loud, or any singer or musician who gets carried away in his or her flamboyance, actually takes attention away from the One we are supposed to be worshiping.

Many churches have dealt with this generational issue by having separate "traditional" and "contemporary" services with music that appeals to the different age groups. This has met with some success, but I think there is great value in trying to keep the various generations together whenever possible. Young people need to see the example of the older saints; their love for the Lord and the dignity and sincerity with which they express that love. And those who are mature in the Lord need opportunities to develop relationships with younger believers as an inroad to disciple them in the faith.

It *is* possible to have worship services that bless congregants of all ages. I have seen it done in a "mega-church" that seats nearly 3,000 people. I have been amazed during the worship time at how the young people stand near the platform singing their hearts out with their hands raised in praise to the Lord. And the older people, while usually more reserved, are clearly being blessed by the time spent expressing their love to God in song. The music is contemporary and the worship leaders are young, but it is not uncomfortably loud and none of the people on the platform draw attention to themselves with their antics. By their actions they show that it is all about God, just as it should be. And this is one of the reasons the church has shown remarkable growth over the years.

CARELESS COMPROMISE

One other thing that bears mentioning is that our actions dim the light of Christ when they are tainted by compromise. During the time I was writing this book, a Christian singer who had gained significant popularity among secular audiences was asked a question during an interview on a non-Christian media outlet. She was simply asked if she believed homosexuality was sin. Based on numerous passages of Scripture in both the Old and New Testaments the answer should have been an easy one: "Yes, practicing homosexuality is a sin." But reflective of much of Christianity today, her answer was a disappointing, "I don't know." She went on to say she had a lot of gay friends that she cared about.

Now, nearly all of us have friends and/or loved ones who have admitted to same-sex attractions. But as Christians we should understand that our concern for them should translate into sharing the truth in love. When this Christian singer gave her answer, she lost a tremendous opportunity to use the platform God had given her to express biblical truth to a huge audience that could have transformed lives for eternity.

Were her comments prompted by compromise in an attempt to maintain her widespread popularity? Or was she really ignorant of biblical truth on this subject? In either case, her answer was very discouraging.

If she was trying to hold on to her fame by giving a politically correct answer, then she will have to answer to God someday for denying His truth before men. As Matthew 16:24 says: "Then Jesus said to his disciples, 'If anyone would come after me, he must deny himself and take up his cross and follow me.'"

But if this singer honestly didn't know what the Bible says on the subject, then that was reflective of the sad reality that so many Christians today are simply unaware of the most basic of biblical truths. This woman was in her mid 20's at the time, and had already been in Christian music ministry for several years, so she should certainly have moved beyond the infant stage in her spiritual maturity. Instead, her immature answer (barring an uncompromising, truth-revealing clarification in the future) will have zero positive impact for the Kingdom of God and the individual lives she could have helped to transform.

I've heard compromise expressed from more than one pulpit as well, and from pastors that I would otherwise consider very solid and devout in their service to God. In one case, the pastor was discussing romantic relationships and how to conduct them in a godly way. One piece of advice he gave made my eyes pop open. To unmarried couples, one of his bullet points was: "Hold off on the physical aspect of your relationship as long as possible." What? *As long as possible*? I could imagine many couples who heard those words agreeing together the next time they battled sexual temptation: "We've waited as long as we possibly can, we can't resist any longer." And then they give in to immorality.

Similarly, a different pastor who was speaking on sexuality fell short when he said, "sex within marriage is the best way..." What? The *best way*? There were perhaps 2,000 people who heard this message, many of whom were immature but growing Christians. They needed to hear the biblical truth that sex within the context of marriage between one man and one woman is the *only way* that is acceptable in the eyes of God.

In each of these cases it appeared the pastors were trying not to offend anybody by being too overt in their comments. Both of these men had large and growing churches and maybe didn't want to risk their recent successes by sharing uncomfortable biblical truth. But their compromising language provided just a couple more examples of why Christianity is losing its influence in the culture.

I have a friend who calls this "accommodational theology" because it attempts to make accommodation for the current cultural trends rather than standing firm on the timeless truths found in God's Word. How can believers be salt and light when they don't even know the basic precepts of Scripture, and are often living ungodly lives themselves as a result?

The move toward compromise is also reflected today in many Christian institutions that were once considered very rock solid. I visited a Bible college recently that I was familiar with from the early 1980's. Back then, one of the stipulations in the code of conduct was that modest dress was to be worn by the students at all times as a way of honoring God.

Fast forward basically just a generation later, and this college had added an on-campus swimming pool. There, sunning on lawn chairs, sitting at the water's edge, or walking around, were numerous shapely young ladies wearing tiny bikinis. Of course, there were several male students there as well. I was deeply troubled that the administrators of this school somehow believed this was acceptable.

These college-age men and women were already being bombarded with sexual temptations everywhere they looked, whether in advertisements, entertainment, online, or wherever. Did the administrators really believe the young men who saw these women walking and laying around in a little bit of nothing would somehow be able to maintain pure, godly thoughts? Did they really believe that allowing such a daily flesh-fest on campus was in some way acceptable in the eyes of God? Or was it simply a glaring example of compromise in order to draw more students and money to the campus? And what a terrible witness to any unsaved visitors who would see such proud immodesty at an institution that was supposed to be dedicated to honoring God and raising up the next generation of Christian leaders.

Whenever God elevates individuals into positions of great responsibility, He holds them accountable for how they use that authority — for better or for worse. I pray for the leaders of our Christian schools, and all of those in positions of ministry leadership, that they will resist the temptation to allow our declining culture to dictate what is acceptable in the eyes of God.

CONCLUDING THOUGHT

This chapter points to some of the important ways we are to be set apart as Christians so that we look different and people will want what we have. In 1 Peter 2:9 we as believers are called, "...a chosen people, a royal priesthood, a holy nation, a people belonging to God, that you may declare the praises of him who called you out of darkness into his wonderful light."

Even in a crowd of thousands we can spot a uniformed policeman because of the way he looks, and we know we can go to him for help when we are experiencing trouble. Our actions as Christians should be just as obvious, creating a "wonderful light," so that even among the masses people will know who they can turn to when they face trials and are in need of answers about the most important questions in life.

This is not just wishful thinking. I was talking to a man just one day before writing these words who I'll call Kent. He had a cousin who had lived a very ungodly life. Kent had regularly shared his faith with this man over the years. Then, Kent's cousin ended up stricken with cancer. As this man lay dying in a hospital bed, of all of the people in his life, he summoned Kent into the room and asked everyone else to leave. This was despite the fact that their relationship was at times distant because of the differences in their beliefs and lifestyles.

Because of Kent's loving investment in his cousin over the years, even when it was difficult, this man knew who to look to in his time of desperate need. He called for Kent because he "looked" different, reflecting the wonderful light of Jesus. During their private death-bed conversation, Kent says this man accepted Christ as his Savior and then died a short time later — immediately taking the journey to his heavenly home. Through this true story Kent provided a tangible and unmistakable example that living a life that honors God, including consistently and uncompromisingly sharing the truth in love, really does matter for eternity's sake.

9–ACTIVITIES:
FEEDING FLESH OR FAITH

As we continue in our journey with Christ, it is important that we progress in our level of spiritual maturity and sanctification. We should never stay in a place where the things of the world mean more to us than the things of God.

I'm going to do something in the next three chapters that is rarely done. I'll be talking in specific terms about some of the activities that have gained acceptability among Christians in recent years, despite their questionable nature. I realize that whenever you do that, you run the risk of being accused of being legalistic. But hopefully after reading chapters one and two of this book, you'll understand that my motivation is a love-inspired encouragement toward prudent constraints of our liberty as believers in Jesus.

Before I move on, I think it will be important to lay a little groundwork to establish why I believe that discernment in regard to our activities even matters in the first place. For many who call themselves Christians today, the casual mindset that I talked about previously prevents them from feeling any concern relating to those things that should justifiably bring cause for pause. There is an "almost anything goes" approach in their walk with Jesus. And anyone who would call into question the wisdom of participating in certain activities or behaviors is often looked at as a legalist.

I heard a preacher one time share a story that provided a nearly perfect analogy for how I plan to deal with my concerns. He said his toddler-age daughter somehow got hold of a sharp kitchen knife and was holding it by the blade. Of course he was horrified! He knew if he tried to harshly rip the dangerous object from her, she would likely be seriously hurt with scars that could last a lifetime. And the resultant medical bills and emotional pain would have an ongoing impact on the rest of the family as well. So the better approach was to try to gently convince her to put the knife down and walk away from it for her own good.

The latter approach is the one I will be using in the next three chapters in relation to the activities we participate in as Christians. As we have seen in several examples I shared previously, when gray area activities are addressed by trying to harshly "rip them" from a person's hand, spiritual harm is often the result with "scars" that can last a lifetime. Instead I intend to use a gentle approach, trying to convince believers to voluntarily put down their own dangerous "knives" — whatever they might be — to protect themselves and those who care about them from the potential for serious harm, now and into the future.

LIVING ON THE WHITE SIDE OF GRAY

I have to say, I am not a believer in the phrase "all things in moderation." It seems that activities or behaviors that we condone only in moderation, like gambling or alcohol consumption, are generally the things that I strongly believe should be avoided altogether. Because once you move beyond moderation, they become either dangerous or downright sinful. (I'll make my case for this in the coming chapters. It will be worth reading I assure you!)

Whenever I talk about these types of "disputable matters" as Paul calls them in Romans 14, I like to refer to what I call "gray area hill." Imagine with me a hill with a rather wide, gently rounded peak in the middle, and steep slopes both to the left and to the right. On one side of the hill is sin, or the black side. On the other side is righteousness, or the white side. In the middle of the rounded peak is the gray area, where the issues we will soon be talking about largely reside.

My admonition to you will be to stay consistently on the white side of gray. Because when you are at the top of this hill and you lean toward the black side of the gray, if you start sliding you will end up heading into sinfulness, its consequences, and a result that grieves the heart of God. But if you lean toward the white side and start sliding, then you are safely headed toward righteousness, its blessings, and a result that pleases God.

Occasionally when I have addressed gray areas, people have said, "Why do you focus on things like alcohol consumption and gambling, but you ignore issues such as gluttony? Have you seen how many overweight Christians there are in our churches?"

My response would be that it's not an either/or situation. None of it is good. But there is a stark difference. We have to eat to survive, but we don't have to drink alcohol or participate in gambling to stay alive. So the struggle with obesity can't simply be avoided, it has to be dealt with in more complex ways.

The same principle still applies, however, when it comes to the gray area hill. We have the choice to eat in ways that are unhealthy, leaning toward the dark side of gray. But if we go too far in that direction we will hurt ourselves and those who care about us. Regular overeating can lead to costly health issues, and even premature death, having a painful effect not only on us but our families as well. That is very similar to the result when activities such as alcohol consumption or gambling are taken too far.

THE FROG IN THE POT

The activities I'll be discussing in this chapter aren't generally as addictive as some others, but nonetheless can also be very spiritually destructive. Among them are certain audio and video choices that are gaining increasing acceptability among many who would call themselves Christians.

The common example of the frog in the pot is extremely valid here. The frog happily sits in some water that's in a pot on the stove, even as the temperature is turned up and up. Eventually, the water becomes so hot that the frog dies. But because the temperature increase was so gradual, the frog didn't sense it until it was too late and he was destroyed.

That's the way it is with many entertainment choices. Gradually, popular entertainment has gotten more and more immoral, often without notice – even among Christian audiences. What kind of music, TV shows, and movies are we consuming with our minds? Most of today's sitcoms in particular have gotten so vulgar and graphic that just a decade or so ago even non-Christians would likely have been appalled by what they saw.

It was very different in the early days of television in the 1950's and 60's. Network sensors at that time were very careful about what they allowed across the airwaves. They understood that people of all ages might be watching, so they were vigilant protectors of our children.

For example, in the 1950's sitcoms *I Love Lucy* and *The Dick Van Dyke Show* even married couples were not allowed to be seen in the same bed together; they slept in single beds separated by a nightstand. And there would be absolutely no thought of any unmarried couples bedding down together.

Later, in 1960's sitcoms like *I Dream of Jeannie* and *Gilligan's Island* modesty continued to be enforced. The necklines on Ginger's dresses were never allowed to plunge too far, and care was even taken to cover up the belly buttons of Mary Ann and Jeannie when they were wearing their two-piece outfits.

Even as recently as the 1970's, in the sitcom *Happy Days* — which was racy by the standards of that day — The Fonz wasn't allowed to wear a leather jacket in the earliest episodes because the sensors felt it would encourage potential gang and criminal activity.

So those in charge of television programming have gone from a sense of cultural responsibility just a few short decades ago to an almost anything goes mentality today. And I mean almost *anything*. I have been able to stomach only a few short minutes of most of the recent sitcoms before having to turn the channel. In my limited exposure to these shows I have heard shockingly graphic language relating to, among other things, genitalia and sexual activity.

NOT EVEN A HINT

We as Christians must ask ourselves, "are these types of things acceptable entertainment choices?" Paul writes in Ephesians 5:3-4:

> But among you there must not be even a hint of sexual immorality, or of any kind of impurity, or of greed, because these are improper for God's holy people. Nor should there be obscenity, foolish talk or course joking, which are out of place, but rather thanksgiving.

I have often thought it would be a terrific idea for each Christian to tape these verses to the edge of their television screens. It would be a great reminder that God's standards for His people are set high. The same passage tells us what we should do with such improper entertainment choices. Ephesians 5:7-11 says:

Therefore do not be partners with them. For you were once darkness, but you are now light in the Lord. Live as children of light (for the fruit of the light consists in all goodness, righteousness and truth) and find out what pleases the Lord. Have nothing to do with the fruitless deeds of darkness but rather expose them.

This Scripture says in no uncertain terms that immoral entertainment is *not* to be a part of our lives. Now a person might say, "I only watch or listen, I don't do." But I can guarantee you — what you feed grows. Jesus says in Mark 4:24: "Consider carefully what you hear...With the measure you use, it will be measured to you–and even more."

We are seeing this increasingly in Christian homes today. Examples of immorality in media abound; sex before marriage, unmarried people living together, adultery, homosexuality, and transgenderism. As this type of entertainment is being perceived as acceptable to more and more believers in Christ, we are now seeing the residual effect. There is a significant increase in the number of young people from Christian homes who are being deceived into accepting, and even participating in, these and other sinful behaviors.

Franklin Graham, son of the late evangelist Billy Graham, gave a spirit-realm perspective on how this works in the April 2014 edition of *Decision* magazine: "Sinful entertainment deposits rubbish in the mind, giving Satan a foothold in our lives. Once there, he thrashes around even as we sleep."

FEEDING YOUR FLESH

If you doubt the correlation between the entertainment that is viewed and the resultant behaviors, groundbreaking research was documented in the November 2005 issue of *Pediatrics* magazine involving about 2,000 12- to 17-year-old girls and boys nationwide. The teens were first interviewed in 2001, and then twice more within the next three years. They were asked how often they watched any of a number of popular TV shows at that time which contained significant sexual content.

The results of the study were rather shocking. Among those who viewed such shows regularly, the pregnancy rate was twice as high when compared to those who rarely watched them. Did you catch that? The pregnancy rate wasn't just a little bit higher, it was *twice as high* among those who watched shows containing significant immorality!

Those who become too engrossed in pop culture are even regularly influenced merely by the lifestyles of their entertainment heroes. In the 1960's, the era of *I Dream of Jeannie* and *Gilligan's Island*, only about 8 percent of babies were born into single parent homes. Today, that number is more than 40 percent.

A 2016 study authored by University at Buffalo sociologist Hanna Grol-Prokopczyk drew a correlation between the prominence of births to unwed mothers in the United States and the way lifestyles of celebrities were portrayed. She examined almost 400 cover stories from a magazine that existed almost solely to dig into the personal lives of the rich and famous.

Grol-Prokopczyk found that stories about pregnant, unmarried celebrities from the 1970's were rare. But when they *were* presented they regularly included information about the father and the couple's plans to soon marry. This was found to be true in the magazine's cover stories even as late as the 1980's. But by the mid-1990's, the desire for marriage was rarely mentioned and there was no indication of any problems related to bearing or rearing a child in a single-parent or unmarried home.

There are those who would dispute this finding, using a "what came first, the chicken or the egg?" argument. I have heard it said regularly by those who disagree with the exhortation toward greater consecration that the immoral free-fall in the media is only reflective of what's already happening in the culture. But I would thoroughly disagree. The real-life and on-screen lifestyles of celebrities are nearly always a cultural leader, pulling us in a direction that they would want us to go — which again, nearly always, leads us toward greater immorality.

The examples are often subtle, but effective nonetheless, in sending the message that biblical morals are no longer relevant. I have to admit that some of my personal favorite movies and TV shows through the years have been among those sending this message.

For instance — *WKRP in Cincinnati* (MTM Productions, Inc.) had an episode in 1978 in which quirky newsman Les Nessman was wrongly accused by a baseball player of being gay. The whole episode of course was comically done, with one notable exception. When crass sales manager Herb Tarlik made a derogatory comment about homosexuality, Jennifer Marlowe, the ultra-smart, ultra-beautiful receptionist said, "...so what if he is [gay]? He comes to work, he does his job, he's a fine person. His sex life is his own business."

Now there was a certain acceptability to what she said. For example, this would be similar to having a co-worker who is unmarried and living with their heterosexual lover. In both cases, they are living sinful lifestyles according to the Bible. And neither of them should be fired for this, provided they work for a secular employer in which their sexuality does not put vulnerable people, such as children, at risk. But it didn't take much to realize that there was intentionality behind what Jennifer said — to create a sense of normalcy and acceptability for the gay lifestyle. This is completely contradictory to what the Bible says on the subject. (I address this topic in detail in chapter 8 of my book *Kingdom Invaders*.)

The 1981 movie *On Golden Pond* (Universal Pictures) had a couple of glaring examples of this type of immoral messaging. While sitting in their cabin, the elderly and outspoken Norman Thayer Jr. said to his wife Ethel that one of the "lesbians" across the pond had just died at the age of 90. To this the always wise and rational Ethel said, "Well, she lived a good life." Again, this was a less than veiled attempt to make the gay lifestyle appear completely normal and acceptable, and I might add, without eternal consequence.

Later in the movie, Norman told Ethel that their visiting adult daughter and her boyfriend wanted to sleep together in the same bed at the cabin. And Ethel responded matter-of-factly, "Why not? They're big people..." indicating that it is absolutely normal, and even expected, that unmarried people sleep together once they have established a romantic relationship. Of course, this type of behavior is also not acceptable according to God's Word. (This is addressed at length in chapter 7 of *Kingdom Invaders*.)

A similar message was sent in the Jim Carrey movie *Liar, Liar* (Universal Pictures, 1997). Carrey's character asked his ex-wife at one point in the movie if she was sleeping with her boyfriend. She responded sarcastically, "We have been dating for eight months, what do you think?" The implication was clear, that if you have been seeing somebody that long it would be absurd to think you weren't having sexual relations with them. Of course the viewer is disarmed by the great humor in the movie, but the message is loud and clear just the same — sex is completely normal and acceptable for committed couples, whether they are married or not. This again is completely contradictory to what the Bible teaches.

These are the types of immoral messages that have been almost constantly fed to us for years in our culture, and as I've already mentioned, the results are undeniable. Even among many who would call themselves Christians, biblical morality is now regularly considered outdated — and even ridiculous.

THE "ADDICTION" OF AFFIRMATION

It is quite clear that peer pressure and especially positive affirmation drives a lot of what is considered acceptable in the culture, and sadly, in the Church today. For example, there has been a surge in public praise for those who show acceptance of homosexuality and transgenderism.

Recently, I watched as a pastor from a large, well-known church in New York City was being interviewed on a nationally televised broadcast. The interviewer made sure to prominently mention that this man was not your typical pastor, such as the fact that he wore very visible tattoos. While this in and of itself wouldn't be a...uh..."black mark" on his credibility, what this pastor said certainly was.

When asked whether or not the practice of homosexuality was a sin, he would not simply answer "yes" which would have been in keeping with biblical truth. Instead, he gave an evasive answer saying something like all people are welcome at his church. (True believers indeed welcome all people into their churches, but we must love them enough to eventually and consistently share the truth that continuing to live a life of sin is not an option in the eyes of God.)

This pastor was lifted up by the interviewer as a new breed of enlightened spiritual leader. You can imagine how wonderful this pastor must have felt after receiving such affirmation. The emotional "high" he experienced was probably similar to the feeling an addict gets when he ingests his favored drug.

Conversely, if he had given the biblical answer that no one can practice ongoing sin unrepentantly, regardless of what it is, he likely would have been lambasted as a narrow-minded, bigoted "hater" and would have never seen that TV show again. So you can see why peer pressure and affirmation can be used powerfully by Satan to prevent Christians from speaking out against detrimental, and even unbiblical, practices.

Affirmation has also been a strong driver in the Church's move toward the "social gospel" and away from the true Gospel. It is hard to find any clear-thinking person who would be opposed to feeding the hungry, giving water to the thirsty, providing clothes to the needy, and caring for the sick as instructed in Matthew 25. So those who focus on this aspect of the Christian faith receive great affirmation, from both believers and non-believers alike.

But when you throw in that pesky issue of moving past meeting temporal needs toward sharing the truth that will meet their needs for eternity, that is when the criticism and resistance often starts. And this too comes from both non-believers and those who claim a commitment to Christ. You might hear something like, "We're doing a really good thing here by feeding and clothing these people. Don't make anybody feel bad by forcing your religion on them."

But if the help these people receive only bridges the gap until they spend their eternity in hell, then it is clearly not sufficient. Meeting their needs has to be a means to a more important end; an opportunity to share the real Gospel, that through Jesus they can have their needs met forever. Affirmation for this message is much harder to find, so it has had diminished focus in recent years when compared to the "easy sell" of the social gospel.

Additionally, in the Church today there is an overflow of affirmation for those who are accepting and embracing things that used to be considered spiritually dangerous; many of the things that in my opinion were wisely approached with caution in previous generations. Today, those of us who stand up to such things are often ridiculed – even by other believers.

For instance, I was involved in a friendly conversation a couple of years ago with two young Christian men who I believed to be rather mature in their faith. One of them commented on how young I looked for my age. They both had been heavily involved in the same holiness denomination that I grew up in, so I jokingly made mention that my youthful look came from practicing the teachings of my church — I didn't "smoke, drink, chew, or go with girls who do."

To me, there was humor in mentioning this rhyme that had often been quoted among straight-laced believers. But it was clear that their subsequent laughter came from a belief that I was making fun of my upbringing and the pursuit of holiness that had been advocated by our denomination for decades. But I was serious! I had never partaken of those things that can cause accelerated aging, and I've been truly thankful for a legacy like that.

This is interesting when you think about it. These young men had the mindset which is so prevalent today — that their permissive attitudes made them much more enlightened than the saints that had gone on before. This was despite the fact that they were mocking the very things that had worked effectively in my life to keep me healthy, while noticeably slowing my aging process.

FEEDING YOUR FAITH

I have often heard a question that in and of itself makes a strong case for the argument that popular culture affects the choices we make: If we are not significantly influenced by celebrities, why do companies pay them millions of dollars to represent their products? So it should be understood that if we feed ourselves a steady diet of our worldly culture through television, movies, secular music, etc. then that influence will inevitably grow in our lives.

On the other hand, if we regularly dish up healthy servings of those things which are wholesome and righteous, that also grows. I can personally testify to this fact.

There was a time in my life when I wanted to serve the Lord but there were many things that were diverting my attention away from Him. I was only going through the motions as a Christian, while at the same time feeding myself a diet of questionable music, TV, and movies (some of which I just mentioned).

But as I wrote earlier, I came to a point where my marriage was falling apart and I appeared to be losing everything that I held dear. In that period of brokenness I recommitted my life to the Lord, and made the choice to become more disciplined in the way I lived out my faith. I began to discover that the more I focused on the things of God, the more of it I wanted.

From time to time I have heard young people in particular say things like "church is boring" or "Bible study is boring." Then they say they would rather stay home and watch their favorite show on TV or visit with friends rather than go to church. There was a time that I could relate to that. But not anymore.

As we continue in our journey with Christ, it is important that we progress in our level of spiritual maturity and sanctification. We should never stay in a place where the things of the world mean more to us than the things of God. Trust me, if you make the conscious choice to prioritize the Lord in your life then your desire for Him will grow. As James 4:8 says: "Come near to God and he will come near to you." I find now that my favorite forms of entertainment include good sermons, and books, videos, and conferences that focus on spiritual growth. And I'm sure the same can happen for you.

CONCLUDING THOUGHT

As I briefly said at the beginning of this chapter, Paul characterized many of the issues that Christians don't necessarily agree on as "disputable matters" in Romans 14. The reality is, no matter how strongly I feel about these issues not everybody is going to agree with me. But as I bring this chapter to a close, I'd like to leave you with a couple of thoughts to ponder.

There are some very good questions to ask yourself that should help in gauging the acceptability of the activities that are a part of your life. When Jesus returns, would you want to be caught listening to, or watching, or participating in what is occupying your time? 1 John 2:28 says: "And now dear children, continue in him, so that when he appears we may be confident and unashamed before him at his coming."

More importantly, would it bother you to think that what you're doing at any given time might be grieving Him? In Philippians 4:8-9 it says:

Finally, brothers, whatever is true, whatever is noble, whatever is right, whatever is pure, whatever is lovely, whatever is admirable–if anything is excellent or praiseworthy–think about such things. Whatever you have learned or received or heard from me–put it into practice. And the God of peace will be with you.

Yes, the types of things mentioned in this passage should not only occupy our minds, but should be "put into practice" in the activities that are a part of our lives.

One final question I would encourage you to ask yourself: "Do my activities move me closer to Jesus and His righteousness or farther away?" Paul writes in 2 Timothy 2:22: "Flee the evil desires of youth, and pursue righteousness, faith, love and peace, along with those who call on the Lord out of a pure heart."

As in the example of the "gray area hill," God wants us to flee temptation and pursue righteousness so that we don't fall into sin that grieves Him, brings disrepute to His Kingdom, and leads to painful consequences. In all of the activities we participate in, we should make sure we do them — or avoid them — with the thought of honoring God always foremost in our minds.

10–ACTIVITIES:
THE GRAY AREA GAMBLE

Today, a person only has to take a quick look at the moral free-fall in the culture to see that the "almost anything goes" mentality adopted by a significant number of Christians in recent years is not working — our light has dimmed and our salt has lost its flavor.

As I mentioned way back in chapter 1, I try to take my neighbor's dog Riley for a walk each evening. But that gets a little difficult during the winter because it gets dark so early that time of year in northern Minnesota. I don't dare take Riley out on our country road in the dark; it would be far too dangerous. So at those times I have to walk alone.

On one of those crisp, cold nights when I began my walk, I looked up into the sky and it was perhaps as pretty a sight as I had ever seen. God's creation never ceases to amaze me with its beauty! It's difficult to describe, but there was a thin layer of clouds with intermittent patches of clearing. Through one of those openings in the clouds I could see a crescent moon and a very bright star that I assumed was the planet Venus. In other openings were a large number of other stars that were shining brightly. Their light created a silver lining on each of the clouds that was absolutely magnificent.

This celestial show got me thinking well beyond the moment. I was feeling so blessed to be living in such a beautiful place, and in a country that provided an extraordinary safety and freedom that so few people had experienced — either then or at any time throughout human history.

But then a sad thought hit me. Even if someone in another country could see such a beautiful sky, would their ability to appreciate it be hindered by a reality for them that included desperate poverty or oppression? Or how about someone right down the road from me. Would they be unable to embrace the beauty of the moment because they lived in a home filled with ongoing contention or abuse?

It occurred to me then that just as only a relatively small number of people had the opportunity to really appreciate what I was experiencing at that moment, there was also only a comparatively small number of people in spiritual terms who actually had tasted the glory of salvation through Jesus Christ.

God has rewarded believers in His Son with amazing blessings. That beautiful sky I was seeing provided a terrific example. Many more breathtaking moments such as that will be ours to enjoy for now, and for a thousand years during the Millennium when there will be no sin-driven distractions to hinder the experience. And then after that, a peace-filled, pain-free eternity with our Father in a new heaven and new earth.

Now please think about this for a moment. What should we do considering all of these amazing blessings He has given to us? Should we simply take advantage of a heavenly Father who gives, and gives, and gives some more? Or should it be understood that with such extraordinary blessing comes immense responsibility to give in return? We certainly could never return to God anything equal to what He has given to us. But what we *can* give is our complete devotion, bringing praise to Him in all we say and do, making our lives a living "hallelujah."

FROM PLANKS TO SAWDUST

One of the most common methods used today to silence Christians who are encouraging others toward a complete devotion to God is to tell them not to be judgmental. "Do not judge, or you too will be judged" are well-known words of Scripture among Christians and non-Christians alike. This is a comment Jesus made as recorded in two of the Gospels, Matthew 7:1 and Luke 6:37. It sounds pretty cut and dried — live and let live; you take care of your relationship with God and I'll take care of mine. But to get a proper understanding of what this actually means, we have to put it into context with the rest of Scripture. Continuing in Matthew 7, Jesus says in verses 3-5:

> "Why do you look at the speck of sawdust in your brother's eye and pay no attention to the plank in your own eye? How can you say to your brother, 'Let me take the speck out of your eye,' when all the time there is a plank in your own eye? You hypocrite, first take the plank out of your own eye, and then you will see clearly to remove the speck from your brother's eye."

First of all, notice that Jesus is using a common Hebrew practice of hyperbole, or obvious exaggeration, to make an important point. He is comparing the smallest piece of wood, a speck of sawdust, to the largest, a plank. What Jesus is saying is important because being wrongly judged can be very painful.

As an example, let's say a man, his wife, and two young sons are always late for the Sunday morning services at their church. After seeing this go on for several months, one of the church board members who has a pet peeve for tardiness has had enough. After a service, he calls the couple aside and harshly condemns them for showing up late and being a distraction week after week.

What the board member didn't know is that the man had gotten a new job several months ago which required him to work overnight Saturday into Sunday. Because of the hours he worked, there was no way the family could make it to the Sunday morning services on time. But the man, as exhausted as he was when he came home from work, wanted to set a good example for his sons so he and his wife agreed it was important to make the effort to go to church, even if it meant being late. So in effect, the couple was wrongly judged after actually trying to go the extra mile to do right in the eyes of God. You can imagine how much ongoing hurt and damage an incorrect judgment, such as that of the church board member, could have caused.

Second, note in the Scripture we just read that Jesus isn't saying we should *never* make a judgment. He says, "first take the plank out of your own eye." In other words, our primary focus should be on keeping our own spiritual house in order. We must self-examine regularly and commit to a life consecrated to God. Then, when behaviors of concern are revealed in others it is proper for us to address those issues for their own good.

But it is important that we don't judge ignorantly based on wrong assumptions (such as in the example of the church board member). We are only to make judgments based on what is clearly evident. And it is critical for us to understand that we are actually *instructed* to judge sinful behavior. Paul wrote in Galatians 6:1: "Brothers, if someone is caught in a sin, you who are spiritual should restore him gently. But watch yourself, or you also may be tempted."

This passage includes a key point when we confront someone caught up in sinful behavior — "restore him gently." Put another way, share the truth in love. And Paul reiterates Jesus' instruction to self-examine regularly when he says, "watch yourself." Satan loves it when we get self-righteous because pride makes us very vulnerable to temptation and sin (Proverbs 16:18).

Finally, note that both Jesus and Paul are making reference to a "brother," meaning they are talking about conduct relating to fellow Christians. In Matthew 7, Jesus continues His thought relating to judging others. In verse 6 He says: "Do not give to dogs what is sacred; do not throw pearls to pigs. If you do, they may trample them under their feet, and then turn and tear you to pieces." Said another way, trying to correct a non-Christian for sinful behavior is ineffective because they have little capacity for understanding God's truth.

YOU GOTTA EXPECT A DOG TO BE A DOG

When my now deceased dog used to bark and wake me up in the middle of the night because another creature — real or imagined — had come onto our property, it would certainly be annoying. But a phrase I heard once from a congenial southern gentleman would come to mind: "You gotta expect a dog to be a dog." Similarly, when a person who is not yet saved lives a sinful lifestyle, we should remember: "You gotta expect a non-Christian to be a non-Christian."

But it should also go the other way: "You gotta expect a Christian to be a Christian." There really should be something different about the way a person who is redeemed through the blood of Jesus lives his or her life. Simply put, a Christian should "look" different. Today, a person only has to take a quick look at the moral free-fall in the culture to see that the "almost anything goes" mentality adopted by a significant number of believers in recent years is not working — our light has dimmed and our salt has lost its flavor (Matthew 5:13-16). Many of the attitudes, actions, and activities displayed by those who would call themselves Christians have been making it harder and harder to distinguish any difference between them and those who have expressed no faith in Christ at all.

Paul addressed this problem in 2 Corinthians 6:16-7:1:

What agreement is there between the temple of God and idols? For we are the temple of the living God. As God has said: "I will live with them and walk among them, and I will be their God, and they will be my people. Therefore come out from them and be separate, says the Lord. Touch no unclean thing, and I will receive you. I will be a Father to you, and you will be my sons and daughters, says the Lord Almighty." Since we have these promises, dear friends, let us purify ourselves from everything that contaminates body and spirit, perfecting holiness out of reverence for God.

So based on this passage of Scripture, we can see that there is clearly a problem if we, as "temples of the living God," are not distinguishable from non-believers in the way we live our lives. Through Paul, God Himself tells us to "come out from them and be separate," striving as best we can for complete holiness out of reverence for Him.

Unfortunately, too many believers in Christ have an upside down approach to their faith. They decide their choice of activities based on whether or not it is sin, as opposed to a desire to represent God well and advance His Kingdom.

Imagine a boundary I'll call the "sin circle." Outside of that circle is activity that is sinful. Inside is behavior that is not sinful. In the very middle is a dot that represents Jesus. Sadly, many Christians make decisions about the activities they participate in with the idea of staying just inside the sin circle. "How close can I get to sin without crossing the line?" Instead, those who love God and want to honor Him with their lives should strive to move away from the sin line and toward the middle, as close to Jesus as they can possibly get.

The choice to live close to the sin line or close to Jesus is seen by others, and over time the residual effect either moves them away from Jesus, or draws them toward Him. And it should go without saying that staying as close to the middle as possible with Jesus will make it far less likely that we will accidentally cross over the sin line — grieving the Spirit of God, inviting consequences, and possibly damaging our witness.

Earlier, I talked about how our liberty in Christ must be constrained by love. If we don't consider how our behavior affects other people, including the activities that we participate in, then we are practicing a selfish faith in which the residual effect can ultimately be a detriment to the Kingdom.

THE GAMBLING GAMBLE

There are many questionable activities that have gained acceptance in recent years among Christians. Gambling, for instance, is one of those vices that Satan is using to devastate individuals, families, and even society as a whole. It used to be that legal gambling in the United States was pretty much limited to Las Vegas, Nevada, and later Atlantic City, New Jersey. It was largely understood that gambling was a potentially dangerous practice and it was avoided by the vast majority of Americans regardless of their religious beliefs.

But gambling has quickly risen into a socially acceptable activity, even among Christians, in just the last few decades. According to the overcominggambling.com website, two out of three of adult Americans placed some kind of bet in 2007. Some went to a nearby casino, some played the lottery, and others participated in some kind of online gambling. (They often call it gaming, but I will avoid that term because in my opinion gambling is no game.)

The website also has plenty of chilling statistics that prove the insidious and damaging nature of gambling. As of 2008:

- The gambling industry had grown tenfold in the U.S. since 1975

- Fifteen million Americans displayed some kind of gambling addiction

- The average rate of divorce for problem gamblers was *nearly double* that of non-gamblers

- The suicide rate for pathological gamblers was *twenty times higher* than for non-gamblers (in fact, one in five attempted suicide!)

- Sixty-five percent of pathological gamblers committed crimes to support their gambling habit (it's interesting to note that the total number of crimes rose *100 percent* within a thirty mile radius around Atlantic City after their casinos opened)

THE CASINO CON, THE LOTTERY LIE

That last statistic relating to crime reminded me of an example that hit close to home several years ago. At a time when I was not in Christian radio, a co-worker was diagnosed with a life-threatening form of cancer. A friendly colleague I'll call Ken took it upon himself to collect donations from the other employees to help with the medical expenses. But after a while, questions began to arise about where the money had gone. To make a long story short, Ken had a gambling problem and had lost it all at a casino. This well-liked man had been brought to disrepute and shame, committing fraudulent activity because of his gambling addiction. If he had been a Christian, he would not only have brought crippling damage to his own reputation but to the reputation of Christ as well.

Today we often think very casually about places like casinos with all of their pretty lights and excitement. We see the commercials where people are winning money and having a marvelously good time. Then in the evening after a day of gambling, these people eat a wonderful meal at a casino restaurant and go to bed in a nicely-appointed, affordable casino hotel. It all sounds like good, clean fun. And that's exactly the way Satan likes it. Because that deceptive image is the type of thing he is using on a daily basis to destroy lives. Try telling Ken, his co-workers, and countless others that casinos are harmless fun — they know better!

Lotteries are also looked at largely today as harmless, and even beneficial, fun. After all, most of them are sponsored by the government and the money raised is used for worthy causes like school funding or protecting the environment. What could be wrong with that? A real life example might help answer that question.

A story was relayed on a radio station I worked at several years ago of a man who had picked up a carton of milk at a local convenience store to bring home to his family. When he was about to check out, he noticed a sign highlighting the ever-growing jackpot in a government-run lottery. So he turned around, put the milk back, and purchased a lottery ticket instead.

You may say this is just one isolated example. But in my many years of working in radio there is an unscientific rule of thumb we have followed — that every listener complaint represents the feelings of at least 100 other people. Similarly, if the man in this example chose to gamble instead of purchase nutritious food for his family, we can know that he represents a significant number of other people as well.

Some argue that personally they merely purchase the occasional lottery ticket just for fun. If they lose, it's no big deal. And if they win, they smile and spend the prize on a free dinner or something. But please think about the example I just gave. If this man had money to spare, would he have returned the milk in order to be able to purchase the ticket? Of course not. And this verifies what statistics have shown, that the people who spend the most money on lotteries are the ones who are least able to afford it. It's not about fun for them; they are taking the very low-percentage chance that a successful outcome will help them feed their families and pay some bills. Instead, far more often than not, they are left with less money in which to do so.

The man returning the milk is also indicative of how lotteries impact private business. The government has essentially become competition for precious consumer dollars, putting a drain on local economies. That small store lost income on the sale of a product as a direct result of the lottery.

This true life example makes a strong argument that gambling should be opposed by people of very divergent political and philosophical perspectives. In his book, *Gambling: Don't Bet On It*, Rex M. Rogers writes:

> Gambling threatens the moral foundations of the culture. It's a package loaded with hidden economic costs. Gambling is bad for business. It's a made-to-order conservative issue.

> Gambling threatens people sometimes listed among the weaker or more vulnerable in the population: the poor, the elderly, and children. Gambling is a regressive tax. It's a made-to-order liberal issue.[12]

Using spirit-realm thinking, I believe gambling options like lotteries provide the powers of darkness the opportunity to tempt people into irrational behavior, wasting money on an unlikely fantasy. The gambler is seeking to have their needs met apart from God, which is a form of idolatry. Why would we as Christians want to have anything to do with contributing to something like that through our participation?

"FUN" FOR ALL AGES

One final set of statistics from overcominggambling.com that I would like to share is perhaps the most troubling to me. It shows that gambling among young people is rising rapidly. Those who admit to gambling:

- 42 percent of 14 year olds

- 49 percent of 15 year olds

- 63 percent of 16 year olds

- 76 percent of 18 year olds

Consider that — more than three out of four teenagers say they have participated in gambling activities by the time they reach adulthood! And why not? This is a residual effect of growing up with parents who now consider gambling to be just another harmless form of entertainment. But based on the statistics I've already shared, I would encourage Christian parents to raise their children with a proper understanding — that Satan regularly uses gambling to destroy lives and it is best avoided. (If you still doubt this, perhaps you would be willing to examine and absorb the previous statistics on gambling-related divorce, suicide, and crime one more time.)

RESPONSIBLE STEWARDSHIP

It's true that the Bible doesn't say, "thou shalt not gamble." But there is strong scriptural support for avoiding the practice. In 1 Thessalonians 3:10 Paul writes: "If a man will not work, he shall not eat." In other words, we are supposed to work for our income. That is God's idea.

In Matthew 25:14-30 we see the Parable of the Talents in which a master going on a journey entrusted money to his servants. They were expected to invest it wisely. It was a comparison to the Kingdom of God, that while we wait for Christ's return we are to use what He has given us wisely. We are commanded to be good stewards of God's provision; it is a trust from Him.

I would submit that spending God's resources on gambling is not a positive use of that provision. And even though gamblers win once in a while, nearly all lose much more than they win in the end. That's indisputable when you realize the gambling industry in the United States reaps literally billions of dollars a year; money that could be used for far more productive purposes.

While we are on the subject of how we spend our money, I'd like to briefly mention a topic not related to gambling for which Christians regularly disagree. Some say that we should boycott companies and individual businesses that advocate for immoral or otherwise anti-Christian agendas as a way of getting them to reconsider their support.

Other believers have no problem spending their money with these entities. They will often say that if you choose to avoid such companies, then you will have nowhere to purchase anything because all businesses are involved with such activity to a certain extent.

Sadly, this is becoming increasingly close to the truth. Companies are one by one succumbing to political correctness in what they publicly choose to support, theorizing that this will help their bottom line. But this is a key reason I am among those who support boycotting companies that embrace immoral and anti-Christian causes. If there are enough followers of Jesus who will spend their money elsewhere, this will have an impact on the decision making at most companies.

I can say this confidently because back in the 1980's an organization called the American Family Association started calling for boycotts of companies that were blatantly running afoul of biblical morality. The AFA was founded by Don Wildmon, a humble Mississippi preacher. He shared his message wherever possible, including Christian radio and television. Believers were enlightened to what these companies were doing, and the result was hundreds of thousands of people who responded by spending their dollars elsewhere. The companies noticed, and many of their policies were changed to reflect a more Christ-friendly approach to business.

At that time, Christians would also join together in boycotting companies that sponsored TV programs that were grossly immoral. This again proved to be a very effective tactic for keeping filth out of the nation's living rooms, and as a result, the minds of the populous as a whole.

The obvious residual effect was a culture that was more honoring and accepting of biblical morality and truth. The products sold, the advertising used to sell them, and where the advertising dollars were spent reflected respect for Christians and the God they represented.

Unfortunately, today things are very different. As the culture shows an increasing disdain for biblical morality, companies are regularly jumping on the bandwagon to endorse that which is an affront to God.

As an example, in 2013 two Fortune 500 companies in my home state openly endorsed the legalization of so-called gay marriage. One of them even sold shirts proclaiming the support, and the money raised through their sale went to organizations that advocated for same-sex "marriages." This same company for decades had funneled "charitable" money to pro-abortion causes. The other company not only endorsed the legalization of homosexual "marriage," but had been putting their money where their values were by sponsoring a gay pride parade for many years.

More recently there have been companies which have indi-rectly — and in some cases directly — been critical of law enforcement authorities. And one company even began airing advertisements that have been critical of males who actually (say it isn't so) exhibit masculinity!

Would businesses such as these support such causes if they knew it would hurt their profits? Based on what I saw in the 1980's, probably not. But because Christians over the years have appeared to lose their collective will to oppose such moves, companies now know they can do these things with economic impunity.

The anti-Christian impact is clearly evident, and literally self-feeding. As the culture slides more and more toward the acceptance of immoral beliefs, the businesses attempt to tap into that sentiment as a way of increasing profits. As a result they pour millions of dollars into advertising and products that embrace those beliefs, effectively providing a significant source of funding that hastens the moral free-fall.

Have we run out of options for decent, God-honoring companies today? Perhaps in some sectors the answer is "yes." But my personal recommendation on this is the same as with every other aspect of the Christian life. I would encourage you to honor the Lord in the best way you can. If you are aware of a business that is blatantly operating in a way that dishonors God, then I would urge you to refrain from spending your money with them as long as another option is available. And if you are put off by the concept of a "boycott," then I would recommend you think of it in terms of a "buycott" – choosing to buy from those companies and businesses that are culturally responsible and Christ-friendly in their practices.

We are not going to be aware of all the undesirable practices companies are involved in. But I encourage you to respond to what you do know. Someday we will have to answer to God for how we spent our money, and I know that I truly want to hear Him say "well done."

NOT VERY NEIGHBORLY

This brings us full-circle back to the topic which started this conversation — gambling. As a final thought, we are told in various passages of Scripture that we are to love our neighbors as we love ourselves. When it comes to gambling, the fact of the matter is that any gain we get comes from the losses of others — sometimes tragically as we saw in the true-life story of Ken. That doesn't appear to me to be a very good way of loving our neighbors as ourselves.

Again in his book, *Gambling: Don't Bet On It*, Rex M. Rogers says: "In places where gambling is legal, pathological gambling is also higher. Pathological gambling is more extreme than problem gambling."[13] As of this writing, an estimated 2 million U.S. adults meet the criteria as pathological gamblers. Another 4 to 6 million are considered problem gamblers. That means up to 8 million homes in America are facing the painful discord of crippling financial challenges, and the statistics we have already seen show that many of these families and lives will eventually end up irreparably broken apart.

So my question is this: Just because certain forms of gambling are legal, and just because you personally may not have a problem with gambling, does that make it OK? Is it loving your neighbor as yourself when you participate in an activity, and inject money into an industry, that directly contributes to the destruction of another's well-being?

Considering all of these things — the addictions, the destroyed lives, the spiritual implications — it should be clear this is an issue that really matters to God. As Paul says in 1 Corinthians 10:23-24:

"Everything is permissible"–but not everything is beneficial. "Everything is permissible"–but not everything is constructive. Nobody should seek his own good, but the good of others.

Gambling is among the great examples of gray areas that are best avoided because they are neither "beneficial" nor "constructive." And it should be quite evident that gambling is all about seeking our own good, and not the good of others.

CONCLUDING THOUGHT

There is a Scripture verse that probably most directly addresses the topic of gambling. In Proverbs 12:11 it says: "He who works his land will have abundant food, but he who chases fantasies lacks judgment." This was an exhortation by the wise author of Proverbs, inspired by the Holy Spirit, to put in a good days work for your money instead of hoping for riches that you did not earn. And "he who chases fantasies," in the context of this passage, is the perfect definition of a gambler. He is described as a person who "lacks judgment."

One more quote from Rex M. Rogers' book, *Gambling: Don't Bet On It*, seems a very fitting way to end this chapter:

> Gambling is fundamentally contradictory not only to biblical teaching of individual stewardship and divine sovereignty but also to the socially borrowed Christian values that made this country strong — the Protestant work ethic, individual value and responsibility, and rationality. Why aren't Christians pointing people away from superstition and toward the supernatural?[14]

11–ACTIVITIES:
IMPAIRED JUDGMENT

My request — my plea — to my brothers and sisters in Christ is that you consider the potential damage down the road of participating in questionable activities; if not to you, to those you care about who might be along for the ride.

S hortly before writing this chapter, I was sitting at a stop-light on a city street when I began to hear a frightening noise that was growing in its intensity. It was a deep rumbling that caused my minivan to vibrate, and I variously thought it sounded like thunder and felt like a mild earthquake. It soon became clear that this sensory explosion was nothing more than a very expensive sound system in an approaching vehicle with the bass and volume cranked.

As this vehicle stopped next to me, my van literally shook. (I'm not exaggerating any of this.) The driver had every right to blast his sound system as loud as he wanted; his windows were shut so I don't believe he was breaking any noise laws. But as the light turned green and he drove away, all I could think was, "this guy is going to be deaf even before he gets to his destination!" And I was very concerned about the welfare of any other occupants of that vehicle, particularly if there were children inside.

If this driver was someone I knew and cared about, like one of my daughters for instance, I would ask her — even plead with her — to reconsider what she was doing for her own good. It may not have seemed like a problem then, but in the not-too-distant future she would very likely regret the choice she had made. Something of great value — her hearing — may have ended up being gone, never to be recovered.

The same can be said for so many gray area activities. Yes, we have significant freedom to do what we want within certain parameters. But there are many things that are quite simply very unhealthy for us — mentally, physically, and/or spiritually. Again I'll share what Paul wrote in 1 Corinthians 10:23: "'Everything is permissible'–but not everything is beneficial. 'Everything is permissible'–But not everything is constructive." My request — my plea — to my brothers and sisters in Christ is that you consider the potential damage down the road of participating in questionable activities; if not to you, to those you care about who might be along for the ride.

ALCOHOL: AMERICA AND BEYOND

One of the activities of greatest spiritual concern to me is the widespread acceptance, and even embrace, of alcohol consumption among believers today. Now I realize that my conviction may differ greatly from yours on this point. It is my understanding that even the great reformer Martin Luther operated a brewery, so I certainly will be fighting an uphill battle with many of you as I discuss my concerns about this particular activity. And as I've mentioned several times already, I come from a holiness background and drinking alcohol was a primary no-no.

So I have spent a significant amount of time studying the issue to determine what my personal conviction should be on this matter, and whether or not it is something I should battle against. I came to realize that alcohol has destroyed the lives of countless individuals and families over the years, and even the cost to whole societies has been dramatic. I believe it is indeed a battle worth fighting!

152

Just as God hates divorce (Malachi 2:16), I have come to hate alcohol consumption. God doesn't hate or condemn the person who is divorced — actually just the opposite. He hates divorce because of the deep pain it causes to the beloved people who are affected by it. Similarly, I don't hate or condemn the person who drinks. I just hate alcohol because of the deep pain it has caused, and continues to cause, in the lives of multitudes of people.

Some shocking statistics compiled by the National Institute on Alcohol Abuse and Alcoholism emphasize the point:

- Nearly 80,000 people die each year in the U.S. from alcohol-related causes (some reports say the number is closer to 88,000)

- In 2012, 24.6 percent of U.S. adults reported that during the previous month they had engaged in binge drinking (defined as five or more alcoholic drinks on the same occasion) — that's about one in four!

- Deaths related to alcohol consumption among women increased *85 percent* from 1999 to 2017

- More than one in ten children in the U.S. lives with a parent who has an alcohol problem

- About 97,000 U.S. college students are victims of alcohol-related sexual assault or date rape each year

- Another 696,000 college students are violently assaulted by another student who has been drinking

- Globally, alcohol use is the fifth-leading risk factor for premature death and disability, and the *number one* risk factor for those between the ages of 15 and 49

- The World Health Organization estimates that more than 3 million people died in 2012 due to alcohol's damaging effects on the body

Is it becoming clear as to why I believe alcohol consumption is a very bad idea? It is absolutely beyond my understanding why we as a culture, let alone we as Christians, are so accepting of the practice. Need to see more?

-   Alcohol is the number one drug problem in America, with 12 million people struggling with addiction

-   Alcohol consumption is involved in

    -   73% of felonies

    -   73% of child abuse cases

    -   81% of spousal abuse cases

    -   41% of sexual assaults

    -   72% of stabbings

    -   83% of homicides

-   Alcohol-related accidents are the leading cause of death among young people in the U.S.

I hope these multiple statistics are opening your mind to the depth of the alcohol consumption problem, and why I believe we need to reboot our thinking about the issue. By the way, that last statistic relating to young people reminds me of a common but misguided argument I have heard for why we should be more accepting of alcohol consumption in the United States.

It has been a widely-held belief among Americans that because alcoholic beverages such as wine are so commonplace at meals in places like Europe, and since their laws regarding alcohol are generally less stringent, the people there learn at a young age how to drink responsibly. Therefore it is reasoned that our alcohol-related problems in this country would be minimized if we just lost our hang-ups about it.

But detailed research commissioned by the U.S. Department of Justice in 2009 debunked this belief. The study was an attempt to find out if lowering the drinking age in the United States might lead to more responsible behavior among young drinkers.

It proved just the opposite. In a nutshell, the data revealed that a majority of European countries have higher intoxication rates among their young people than do youth from the United States. It also found that in a majority of these countries, a greater percentage of young people reported having been drunk before the age of 13.

Please don't miss this point. Making alcohol consumption more acceptable and mainstream in a society does *not* reduce the prevalence of its abuse among young people. On the contrary, the residual effect is actually quite predictable; creating a greater legitimacy for alcohol produces a culture full of young people who get drunk more often, and at an earlier age.

THE CURIOUS ACCEPTANCE OF ALCOHOL

I had a strong conviction against alcohol consumption before I worked as a sheriff's dispatcher for eight years in the 1990's. But after seeing the devastation it caused night after night, my conviction deepened. Confirming the crime statistics I quoted a moment ago, the vast majority of serious calls we took were alcohol related. From child and spousal abuse, to sexual assaults and sexually immoral behavior, to deadly traffic crashes, alcohol was a major factor most of the time.

Later during my time as a radio news director, I decided for a one-year period to make a copy of each of the alcohol-related stories that came across my desk. There ended up being hundreds of stories in a pile of paper more than an inch thick where lives were directly or indirectly damaged or destroyed by the consumption of alcohol. And sadly, that included a tragic increase in the number of college students who were dying from alcohol poisoning that particular year. There was also a shocking number who died after going to binge parties on or near campus. These young people with promising futures would walk away only to disappear, drown, freeze to death in the winter cold, or meet up with some other awful fate.

According to a report by the Centers for Disease Control and Prevention published in July 2014 in the journal *Preventing Chronic Disease*, 1 in 10 deaths among American adults between the ages of 20 and 64 is attributable to alcohol consumption. Dr. Karl Benzio is a psychiatrist at the Lighthouse Network, an addiction and mental health counseling helpline. Commenting on the CDC report in a July 7th, 2014 e-newsletter, Dr. Benzio said some of these deaths are due to long-term alcohol use, including breast cancer and liver and heart disease. Other deaths are related to the immediate consumption of alcohol, such as violence, alcohol poisoning, and automobile accidents.

Dr. Benzio acknowledged that alcohol is often used as a way of relaxing after a hard day, or as a way of dealing with stressful situations. He said, "Alcohol does work as a tranquilizer or sedative to lower the heart rate and blood pressure." But he then added, "Research clearly shows the dangerous effects of alcohol on every system of the body...many who use alcohol in a casual manner are putting a toxin into their bodies and dealing with the cumulative effect of that toxin on their brains and all of their systems." He went on to say that the top three causes of death for those under the age of 21 are car accidents, homicides, and suicides, and that "alcohol plays a major role in all three."

Despite all of the individual and cultural devastation caused by alcohol consumption at any age, it boggles my mind that we as a society will tolerate it. If anything else had such a destructive influence it would be banned from our midst. But alcohol gets a free pass — an example of its addictive, and I believe spiritual, grip. (More on that later.)

AN ALCOHOL SUBSTITUTE

I'd like to pretend just for a moment that some innocuous beverage has taken the place of alcohol. I'll use grape soda in a hypothetical example. It will be my attempt to show how the unquestioned acceptance of booze in society is actually quite bizarre. I'll do this by using the plethora of statistics I've already mentioned and incorporating them into a fictional news story:

> The U.S. Centers for Disease Control and Prevention has recently uncovered a serious health threat. It has been discovered that grape soda is responsible for about 80,000 deaths every year across the country. This is due to health issues such as breast cancer, and liver and heart disease, that are known to be attributable to grape soda. Other deaths related to the consumption of the beverage include violence and automobile accidents. And tragically, the top three causes of death for those under the age of 21 are car accidents, homicides, and suicides, and the CDC says grape soda plays a major role in all three.
>
> College campuses have become very dangerous places due to the prevalence of its consumption as well. About 97,000 U.S. college students are victims of grape soda-related sexual assault or date rape each year. And another 696,000 college students are violently assaulted annually by another student who has been drinking grape soda. Sadly, this is just the tip of the iceberg when it comes to the violent crimes influenced by grape soda consumption. The beverage is a factor in 73% of felonies across the nation, 73% of child abuse cases, 81% of spousal abuse cases, 41% of sexual assaults, 72% of stabbings, and 83% of homicides.

Because of the widespread and varied dangers associated with the consumption of grape soda, and thanks to pressure from the literally hundreds of thousands of victims who have been pressing for action, the CDC has proclaimed a public health emergency and has ordered an absolute ban on grape soda. The agency has ordered all retailers to discontinue selling the beverage immediately and dispose of all remaining stock.

I pray that this fictional story causes many to consider a new perspective on this issue. Any other product that was so damaging to individuals and society would have been expelled from the country long ago. This whole story is completely reflective of the true-to-life effects of alcohol consumption in America, with the exception of course of the last paragraph; if only such a nationwide ban was true for alcohol as well. But that has been tried once, and we know the result thanks to the darkened heart of man.

I have often pondered what would have been the result if the 1930's alcohol prohibition in the U.S. had remained the law of the land. How many children would have been spared the devastation of a broken home, or protected from the painful tragedy of abuse or neglect at the hands of an alcoholic parent? How many families would have been kept from the ravages of poverty had an alcoholic father not lost his job, or succumbed to illness, or been killed in a drunken traffic accident? How many women would be living in emotional freedom rather than trying to piece their lives back together after the pain of a sexual assault at the hands of a drunken attacker. And how many people would still be alive today had they not been killed by drivers who got behind the wheel after a few "innocent" drinks?

WHO NEEDS SAFETY?

In nearly every other way, it seems we as a culture are putting a greater emphasis on safety. For example, when I was a kid in the 1960's and 70's we never wore bicycle helmets. Like my favorite comedian, Jeff Allen (who is about my age) says, "it would have been more dangerous to wear the helmet because the other kids would have pelted you with rocks!" A few decades ago, hockey players didn't wear helmets (and some goalies didn't even wear masks). It's amazing that only one NHL player ever died from injuries sustained in a game. Trampolines today have protective netting around them, modern cars have airbags upon airbags, many people are pushing for greater gun control laws, and on and on it goes. You get the point — we live in a safety-first society like never before.

Yet when it comes to alcoholic beverages, many safeguards are actually being removed. In recent years in my home state of Minnesota, the law was changed to allow bars to stay open an hour longer each night, "craft" brewers were given more freedom to produce their product, and the sale of alcohol on Sundays was made legal for the first time. (I believe this last one also speaks to the greater issue of Sundays no longer being considered the Lord's day in our culture, but rather, just basically another Saturday.) This was all despite the fact that a full one in seven licensed drivers in Minnesota already had at least one DWI on their record!

BEWARE OF THE ROARING LION

With all of this in mind, it is especially hard for me to understand why we are so accepting of this damaging drug — not just in secular culture, but in the Christian community as well. Not only is there tangible, empirical evidence for the destructive nature of alcoholic beverages, but when you look at it from a spirit-realm perspective alcohol is also clearly one of Satan's favorite tools for destroying lives.

It is a proven fact that alcohol lowers inhibitions. In other words, it makes the drinker more likely to give in to temptation. So why, *oh why*, are we as believers so willing to give it a passing grade of acceptability? I don't know about you, but I do not want anything in my life that will make it easier for me to sin.

I know there are pastors who share my concerns, but are not sure how to approach the issue with their congregations. How do you encourage your flock to stay away from alcohol without making it sound like a legalistic mandate? We dealt with this in a church I was attending several years ago, and as a board member at the time I came up with some suggested wording for our bylaws that I felt struck the right balance:

> "It is strongly recommended that members avoid all alcohol consumption due to its great potential to cause physical and/or spiritual harm."

This simple statement removes the difficult to manage requirement that church members abstain from alcohol, while at the same time sends an unambiguous message that its consumption is something that legitimately causes great concern.

I felt really good about my decision to encourage such a stance by our church just a short time later. A teenage girl who attended the youth group at a neighboring church was killed in an automobile crash, and toxicology results found that she had been drinking alcohol before getting behind the wheel. My heart broke as I heard the news. I can remember wondering if her church had ever conveyed a message about the dangers of alcohol before her tragic death. And then I pondered, "what if she had been attending our church at the time of the crash?" As part of the leadership team, I can recall thinking that I would never have been able to forgive myself if I had not taken a strong, heartfelt stance in front of the congregation imploring abstinence from alcohol consumption.

There are certain popular sayings, even among Christians, that I simply don't agree with. One of them is, "do all things in moderation." I believe this applies to most things, but certainly not to this particular topic. Now, I realize that the Bible doesn't say something like, "thou shalt not drink one beer" or "thou shalt not have one glass of wine with a meal." But I would challenge you to find even one alcoholic who knew he would eventually have a problem when he took that first drink.

A testimony I heard on our radio network a few years ago provided a good case in point as to why I believe total abstinence is prudent. The man identified himself as Jeff. He gave the testimony after going to Adult and Teen Challenge, a highly-successful, Christian-based drug and alcohol treatment program.

Jeff said he had his first taste of alcohol with his wife on their honeymoon. It was champagne, a "classy" alcoholic beverage largely reserved for such special occasions. After just one sip, Jeff said that neither he nor his new bride liked the taste so they dumped it out. But he said he felt something that night and never forgot the sensation of the champagne sliding down his throat. Using spirit-realm thinking, it was pretty clear that the powers of darkness had seized on the opportunity and bombarded Jeff with temptation. He couldn't get the thought out of his head, and starting with that one drink Jeff began traveling down a road to alcohol addiction.

It nearly ruined his marriage before he was introduced to the life-changing power of Jesus Christ through the Adult and Teen Challenge ministry. This was a glaring example of an important truth from God's Word. 1 Peter 5:8 says: "Be self-controlled and alert. Your enemy the devil prowls around like a roaring lion looking for someone to devour."

What a great word picture! When we are not alert to potential danger, as in Jeff's example, Satan is watching like a hungry lion for an opportunity to pounce. That is why I believe there are so many warnings in the Bible related to the consumption of alcohol — Proverbs 20:1, 23:20, 23:29-32, Isaiah 28:7-8, and Ephesians 5:18 among them. I believe all of these red flags strengthen the case that the best approach for God's people would be that they just simply avoid alcohol consumption altogether.

In fact, there are examples in both the Old and New Testaments of those who were instructed by God not to consume alcohol as a way of setting themselves apart for His service. The priests were given this admonition in Leviticus 10:8-9:

Then the Lord said to Aaron, "You and your sons are not to drink wine or other fermented drink whenever you go into the Tent of Meeting, or you will die. This is a lasting ordinance for the generations to come."

In Numbers 6, abstinence from alcohol was among the ways the Nazirites were told to separate themselves unto the Lord. And in Luke 1:15, the parents of John the Baptist — before he was even born — were instructed by God that he should never "drink wine or other fermented drink."

When you consider these passages, it would appear that God considers alcohol consumption incompatible with His highest ministry standards. It makes avoiding alcohol seem less an issue of legalism vs. liberty, and more about the pursuit of a greater consecration unto the Lord.

AN ISSUE OF STUMBLING

Most people that I talk to who defend the practice of a particular vice such as alcohol consumption will say they have no temptation to go beyond what is safe. But even when it is believed that we personally will not have a problem, we must consider how our use of these things — and therefore our endorsement — may affect our weaker brothers and sisters in Christ. Paul talks about this in Romans 14:19-21:

Let us therefore make every effort to do what leads to peace and to mutual edification. Do not destroy the work of God for the sake of food. All food is clean, but it is wrong for a man to eat anything that causes someone else to stumble. It is better not to eat meat or drink wine or to do anything else that will cause your brother to fall.

I recently talked with a father whose son, many years before, had to go through alcohol treatment at an age not much older than a college student. When his son was a child, the father would occasionally put some wine in the refrigerator to drink with a meal. Decades later after a well-lived life, the father told me he had few regrets. But he said very sincerely that if there was one thing he could go back and change in his life, it would be that he would never have brought alcohol into his home. Granted, this son could still have had issues with alcoholism regardless of what his father did. But nonetheless, this true-life example emphasizes how critical it is that we take into consideration our weaker brothers and sisters before we choose to participate in anything that may be a stumbling block to them.

Another man I talked with said he always had a beer after physical activity such as mowing the lawn because "nothing quenched his thirst better." He said he had no problem with alcohol addiction and therefore had no intention of quitting. However, a few years later his son apparently *did* have a problem with it as evidenced by the fact that he had received several minor consumption charges, numerous other alcohol-related clashes with the law, and a series of toxic relationships fueled by alcohol abuse. And it's worth noting that many times the very people who told me they personally had no problem with drinking ended up intoxicated sometime thereafter, including the man I just mentioned.

THAT WONDERFUL WEDDING WINE

Often when I take my stand against alcohol consumption, I will hear those who oppose my position say, "Well, Jesus' first miracle was to turn water into wine so drinking alcohol must be OK." They are referring to the wedding at Cana in John 2. It sounds like a slam-dunk argument in their favor. But there is a lot more here than meets the eye, including the fact that we can't interpret this event entirely from our modern, Western perspective.

First of all, a couple of words from the original language of the New Testament have to be properly understood. The Greek word for wine, oinos, was used in a continuum for any beverage that came from the juice of grapes. It does not make any differentiation between fresh-squeezed grape juice and fully-fermented wine.

Often the grape juice of that time was stored as a condensed grape "honey" that would later have water added to it. According to various ancient religious and secular writers, the "choice" wine in John 2:10 would be referring to the sweeter grape "honey" that had just been hydrated. There would be virtually no fermentation at this point. We would know this because the fermentation process would break down the sugars in the grape juice making it less sweet as it aged.

Another Greek word we need to look at in John 2:10 is methusko, which is translated in the New International Version of the Bible as "too much to drink." In our Western culture, this has regularly been assumed to mean "got drunk." While methusko can mean "become drunk," it can also mean "filled or satisfied" without reference to intoxication. With this understanding, the New American Standard Version probably has the most appropriate translation when it says, "when the people have drunk freely."

Keeping these things in mind, we can now put a crucial question to the test. Did Jesus sin when He turned the water into wine? Of course not. The Bible tells us that Jesus never committed a sin, the indisputable qualification to be our Savior.

Now think about this. If oinos was fermented wine, and methusko meant that the wedding guests were drunk, then Jesus would have been in effect supplying booze to a drunken wedding party. Since Jesus was without sin, we can draw the very reasonable conclusion that He would not have contributed to the drunkenness of His weaker brothers and sisters in this way.

So the common Western understanding about this miracle simply doesn't pass the smell test. With all of the pertinent facts considered, it seems clear that the fermentation in the wine Jesus created — if it had any at all — would have been so low that the partakers' cells would have drowned before they could have gotten drunk.

A TIP FOR TIMOTHY

Another passage of Scripture that has often been used to justify alcohol consumption is 1 Timothy 5:23, where Paul instructs the young pastor Timothy: "Stop drinking only water, and use a little wine because of your stomach and your frequent illnesses." But it would be quite a stretch to consider this an endorsement of the recreational consumption of alcohol.

First of all, it is obvious from this passage that Timothy did not drink wine on a regular basis. Second, I can guarantee that the water in Ephesus where Timothy preached was not purified in the local municipal treatment plant. There may have been impurities in the water that were making him sick.

So Paul instructs Timothy to do what was common at that time in order to safely hydrate the body — drink the fruit of the vine. And just as with the wedding at Cana, Paul was likely referring to wine that had little if any intoxicating qualities. Even if it did, it really wouldn't matter; it had a medicinal purpose (similar to the medicine I take when I have a bad cold). What does matter is that it would be a clear distortion of this verse to use it as justification for consuming alcohol simply for gratification.

Similar to this example from Scripture, I have often heard about studies in recent days touting that a "little" red wine is good for the body because it contains antioxidants which have shown promise in fighting heart disease and cancer. But what you rarely hear is that research studies also suggest that most types of grape juice provide virtually the same benefits. In a post on the renowned Mayo Clinic website from July 18, 2017, Registered and Licensed Dietician Katherine Zeratsky wrote that non-fermented grape products, such as red and purple grape juice, are similarly rich in health-producing antioxidants. And these can be enjoyed without any of the potential consequences related to alcohol consumption.

THE FACADE OF SOPHISTICATION

It's interesting to me that wine is almost always spoken of in glowing terms throughout the culture. I just returned from a popular media-driven fishing event in Minnesota, a state which is known as the "Land of 10,000 Lakes." (Actually there are nearly 12,000 lakes of 10 acres or more in the state, but that number doesn't look as good on a license plate.)

At virtually every restaurant we were taken to as part of the event, "fine wines" were available. It was always presented as the most sophisticated of beverages to consume with a meal. And never far away were the "craft beers," highlighted as a classy, locally-produced option. It began to occur to me that alcohol consumption is such a deeply ingrained part of our culture that it's no wonder much of Christianity has gotten on board with its acceptability, regardless of the spiritual and physical dangers.

This societal love affair with alcohol was perhaps never more glaringly obvious than during the worldwide coronavirus pandemic that ramped up in the U.S. in early 2020. In order to slow the rampant person-to-person spread of the so-called COVID-19 virus, governors throughout the country implemented stay-at-home orders on their citizens. Only businesses that were deemed to offer "essential" services were allowed to stay open. And believe it or not, in many states *liquor stores* joined places such as gas stations, grocery stores, and medical facilities on the list of essential services! Interestingly, in July of 2020 when *Worldometer* had tallied 669 thousand deaths worldwide due to COVID-19, alcohol deaths that year had already surpassed 1.4 million – more than double.

To me this is a very sad commentary about the grip that alcohol consumption has today. That is why I have taken such a significant amount of time here addressing the issue. Because, in addition to the culture, I have seen alcohol negatively affecting Christianity like never before. Satan is using it to topple church-going individuals and families in increasing measure.

I have many dear friends who disagree with my admonition for abstinence, and yet their lives still reflect a sincere devotion to God. This is actually one of the very reasons I bring the encouragement that I do. Because I don't think any one of them wants to do anything, or endorse anything, that would tarnish the reputation of Christ.

In some high-profile examples, the late Glen Campbell, Mel Gibson (of Passion of the Christ fame), and Randy Travis are among just a few of the famous people who had made an outspoken commitment to Jesus and then were disgraced by embarrassing episodes of public drunkenness — and even arrests.

Now, I'm not trying to cast stones at these men. I realize that we all as Christians fall short at times. As 1 John 1:8 says: "If we claim to be without sin, we deceive ourselves and the truth is not in us." But this serves to emphasize my point. Wouldn't it be wise to get the things out of our lives that can bring us, and perhaps others, to the edge of a spiritual cliff?

Time and time again I have seen Satan use alcohol to trip up God's people and bring serious damage to the reputation of the Kingdom. Only God knows how many people have made decisions to reject Jesus because those who called themselves Christians, like those famous examples I just mentioned, succumbed to disgraceful alcohol-influenced behavior.

CONCLUDING THOUGHT

I would encourage you to start thinking about alcohol consumption with a spirit-realm mindset. When you do, it should become clear that there is a real, supernatural evil that surrounds the issue. Do you doubt this statement? Let's take a look at the interesting, well-known verse found in Ephesians 5:18: "Do not get drunk on wine, which leads to debauchery. Instead, be filled with the Spirit."

The implication here is actually fairly obvious. We know from this verse why alcoholic beverages are euphemistically called "spirits." Both alcohol and the Holy Spirit have the ability to strongly influence the behavior of the consumer; one for the bad, the other for the good. But the previous three lesser-known verses lay the foundation for this important point. In Ephesians 5:15-17 Paul writes:

> Be very careful, then, how you live–not as unwise but
> as wise, making the most of every opportunity, because
> the days are evil. Therefore do not be foolish, but under-
> stand what the Lord's will is.

Then the instruction follows: "Do not get drunk on wine." Putting it all together in context, we can see that how we treat alcohol consumption is one prominent and important aspect of being "very careful" with how we live as Christians.

There is no option for a casual approach to the issue. Getting drunk is unwise and foolish, and "leads to debauchery." (The Funk and Wagnalls Dictionary defines this word as "gross indulgence of one's sensual appetites." I would further define it as overt sinfulness.) Conversely, being filled with the Spirit is wise and leads to an understanding of "what the Lord's will is."

The days are evil, and we indeed need to be very careful how we live. If we are serious about the potential salvation of our unsaved friends and loved ones we don't have the luxury of either intentional or "oops" episodes of drunkenness. Those would be lost opportunities to represent Christ well and maybe draw someone to Him. And we never have to worry about any drunkenness, or life-destroying alcoholism, if we do not allow alcoholic beverages to become a part of our lives in the first place.

12 – THE HOLY SPIRIT: OUR STEADFAST ALLY

When we pray in an unknown tongue, the Spirit is praying through us — way beyond our own knowledge of any situation — and in direct conformity with the will of God. That is why the baptism in the Holy Spirit is so powerful.

No book on living victoriously as a "warrior" for the Lord would seem complete without a discussion on the baptism in the Holy Spirit. Unfortunately, what I believe about the doctrine may differ from what you believe. I am going to humbly ask that you please stay with me and read to the end regardless of your current understanding. What I am planning to do in the next two chapters is take a calm, rational, intellectual, and Bible-based look at the subject.

As with nearly everything else I have written so far in this book, I am of no illusion that everybody will agree with me. I am simply going ask you to keep an open mind as I do my best to explain my perspective on the doctrine of the baptism in the Holy Spirit. And then as always, I would encourage you to do what I have to do regularly on biblical matters — pray that God would reveal what His truth really is on the matter. Whether we are in agreement or not by the end of the next two chapters, I want to thank you in advance for taking the time to kindly read what I believe about the baptism in the Holy Spirit.

NOT SEEING IS BELIEVING

Imagine with me if you will that I got into a car crash. I was driving through an intersection on a green light when another vehicle went through his red light. I slammed on my anti-lock brakes but it was too late and I struck his driver's door. Thankfully nobody got hurt, but when the police officer arrived to take the accident report, the description of what happened varied between what I and the other driver said. So the officer began asking a small crowd of curious onlookers if any had witnessed the collision.

One man said he knew what happened. He said that *I* was the one who had gone through a red light and crashed into the side of the other car. Another man said it was clear that I was driving distracted, perhaps by a cell phone, because I smashed into the side of the other vehicle without even slowing down.

Mine was the only accurate description of what happened. Why?

The first so-called witness had actually been around the side of a building and only *heard* the collision. When he went to investigate, he drew his own conclusion about what had just occurred based on evidence that had been incorrectly interpreted. He saw that I had struck the driver's door of the other car and assumed that I was the one who had gone through the red light.

The second "witness" had in reality arrived about five minutes after the crash and based his perception of what happened on the inaccurate comments made by others already at the scene. These people had also not witnessed first-hand what occurred, but came up with their own opinions that fit reality as they believed it to be. Since there were no skid marks thanks to the anti-lock brakes, they assumed I hadn't even tried to stop before the collision and therefore must have been driving distracted.

But what about the other driver? He also experienced the collision just as I had, so why was his assessment so different? Well, the driver had a passenger who realized the impact the truth was going to have on the outcome of the situation, so he started immediately feeding the driver lies about what had happened. The driver had just enough confusion that he bought the lies and began to recount the incident in a way that veered from the actual truth.

A PROBLEM WITH PERCEPTION

This fictional story is meant to highlight what it has felt like in recent years to be someone who has been baptized in the Holy Spirit with the evidence of speaking in tongues. I am a third-generation Pentecostal believer who was born into a family of people who speak in tongues — or put another way — languages they have never learned.

Now, at this moment some of you are probably saying, "That's it! I am not reading another word. Randy is one those heretic pew jumpers!" But please keep reading, even if only due to morbid curiosity. No matter what you may have been taught, when you look at the subject with sincerity I think you'd have to agree there is just way too much written in the Bible about speaking in tongues for it to be considered unimportant, or somehow, not relevant for believers right up to the present time. Almost the entirety of the book of Acts, and significant portions of 1 Corinthians, refer to the issue – first historically, and then with instruction on how to properly put it into practice.

The perception that Pentecostals are somewhat wacko sadly has some merit. To clarify, the *perception* has merit, but not the actual beliefs of Pentecostals. The incorrect perception has been driven largely by certain Christian television hosts — you know, those flamboyant preachers with the wild proclamations and antics that are often accompanied by a request for money. These far-out expressions have all too often been passed off as manifestations of the baptism in the Holy Spirit.

There have also been certain "abuses" inflicted by well-meaning Pentecostals that have turned people off to the beauty and truth of the doctrine. Speaking in tongues is believed by most Pentecostals (including me) to be the initial evidence of the baptism in the Holy Spirit. So when those who have already received this manifestation pray for those who have not, some weird things have happened. Among them, one preacher who jokingly said he received a "tongue-ectomy."

He said when he was young he went forward during a service to pray for the baptism in the Holy Spirit. It took a while, which it often does. This preacher said someone who was trying to help him grabbed his tongue, started wiggling it, and said, "That's it...let it go...just speak forth the language the Holy Spirit is putting into your mind!" And the preacher humorously recalled his next thought: "I *would* speak if you'd just let go of my tongue!" Just for the record, he did begin to speak in a language he had never learned and is today a strong advocate for this wonderful blessing God has made available to us as believers in Jesus.

For some who reject the doctrine of speaking in tongues, these examples I just gave would be similar to the "witness" in my car crash analogy who was around the corner of a building. They have made their own conclusions based on evidence that has been incorrectly interpreted.

Others spurn the doctrine because they have been taught all of their lives that the baptism in the Holy Spirit was intended only for the first century believers to help get Christianity off the ground — or perhaps that any tongues-talking today is only meant for the mission field where people speak another language. These are the predominant beliefs officially taught in many denominations, and are widely heard on most Christian radio shows in the United States. This would be similar to the car crash "witness" who had arrived five minutes after the collision and based his perception of what happened on the inaccurate assessments made by others who also had not actually seen the crash.

And finally there are those who have actually experienced the baptism in the Holy Spirit with the evidence of speaking in tongues but have since turned against the doctrine. This would be similar to the other driver in the car crash analogy. The passenger would represent the powers of darkness that deceive the previously Spirit-filled believer into doubting and rejecting what he had literally experienced himself.

This last example brings to mind a prominent question I had for a long time when dealing with the subject. Why is there so much confusion, even among mature Christians, as to the correct interpretation of this doctrine? In frustration one day, I asked that question of a sister in Christ who had a strong, Spirit-filled prayer life. And her simple response made absolute sense to me. She said since a special supernatural power to witness and live a godly life are among results of the baptism in the Holy Spirit, we know that Satan is going to all he can to bring confusion to the doctrine. I believe she was exactly right!

Maybe you are among those with a negative opinion about the Pentecostal perspective on the baptism in the Holy Spirit due largely to the imperfection of God's people. If so, my encouragement to you would be this: Please don't focus on a little dust in the air when a mighty rushing wind is blowing through.

A HISTORICAL PERSPECTIVE

Jesus himself said in Acts 1:8 just before his ascension to heaven: "But you will receive power when the Holy Spirit comes on you; and you will be my witnesses in Jerusalem, and in all Judea and Samaria, and to the ends of the earth." So certainly, as Kingdom warriors who want to be the most powerful and effective servants of the Lord we can possibly be, we will want to know what it actually means to have the Holy Spirit manifest Himself in this very special way.

I assure you, this discussion on the baptism in the Holy Spirit will not include any hysteria or nonsense. To start with, I'm going to share a very brief history of the modern Pentecostal movement, and then numerous dramatic statistics to show that this particular view on the doctrine deserves serious consideration.

It all started right around the turn of the twentieth century when many people believed the Lord's return was getting very close. There were simultaneous stirrings in the hearts of many people throughout the world to experience the fullness of the Holy Spirit as mentioned in the Bible. This began with a desire for personal holiness and a supernatural power to reach the lost in the last days.

Charles Fox Parham was one of the early church leaders in search of this special "enduement of power." He led a Bible school in Kansas City in which he gave the students an assignment: Discover biblical evidence for the baptism in the Holy Spirit. To this point, there was no uniform agreement on this subject among believers. After completing their assignment, the students concurred that in the Bible the initial evidence for the baptism in the Holy Spirit was consistently speaking in tongues; a language that had not been learned by the speaker. They also agreed that such baptism clothed the believer with power for service.

As 1901 began, several people associated with Parham's ministry began to speak in tongues. But it wasn't until a few years later, at an old two-story building in Los Angeles, that the baptism in the Holy Spirit started becoming the spiritual "shout heard 'round the world." The now famous Azusa Street Revival began in 1906 led by a humble African-American preacher named William Seymour. For three years people came by the thousands from around the country, and even the world, and received the baptism in the Holy Spirit with the evidence of speaking in tongues. Along with it, other manifestations of the

Spirit became common, including healings from diseases and deliverance from addictions and other gripping sins.

Since that time, the growth in the Kingdom of God through the Pentecostal witness has been remarkable. I'm going to share some almost unbelievable examples. To do this, I will unavoidably have to name a few denominations. It is not my desire to demean or glorify any of them; it is merely an attempt to show that there really is something to this amazing gift from God that can only be explained supernaturally.

First of all, let's take a look at the country of Chile. In 1909, when the Pentecostal movement was in its infancy, the Methodists were already established in the South American country. In 2000, they numbered a mere 6,000 or so members. During the same time frame, Pentecostal adherents went from zero to more than 2.3 million.

In nearby Brazil, Baptists were also well established as early as 1912. By 1998, they had reached a respectable 1 million members. However, Pentecostals, which again started at zero, had membership that grew to around 21 million during that period.

In perhaps the clearest evidence of Holy Spirit power, the Assemblies of God — the world's largest Pentecostal denomination — was founded in 1914 as hundreds of pastors who were meeting in Hot Springs, Arkansas embraced the doctrine of the baptism in the Holy Spirit with the evidence of speaking in tongues. (This has been the major distinctive of the denomination ever since). Many other pastors at the gathering, with virtually the same spiritual beliefs, rejected the emphasis on the baptism in the Holy Spirit and proceeded to form the Christian and Missionary Alliance.

In nearly every other way, the two fellowships have been doctrinally the same. But growth has been very different. In approximately the first eight decades of their existence, CMA membership in the United States had risen to about 265,000, while A/G adherents numbered around 2.4 million — nearly tenfold higher. Worldwide through 1992, CMA membership had reached 1.9 million, with the A/G growing to about 25 million.

Let me reiterate — in nearly every other way these two denominations have been doctrinally the same. So what has been the difference? Does the Assemblies of God have better preachers? Or does it have better strategies and programs? Maybe, maybe not. But it would seem obvious that such a dramatic difference in growth couldn't just have happened by the intellect or actions of man. It would have to be supernaturally sourced — the power that comes from the baptism in the Holy Spirit. Just to add an exclamation point to this claim, by 2005 the Assemblies of God reached about 53 million worldwide — more than doubling its membership in just 13 years!

In 2006, 100 years after the Azusa Street Revival began, approximately 600 million precious souls had become part of the body of Christ around the world through the Pentecostal witness. A quick check of the math shows that this averages about a half-million decisions for Jesus every month for a century!

This is an amazing harvest of souls as the Holy Spirit is clearly manifesting Himself like never before in these last days. It is also a fulfillment of the Old Testament prophecy found in Joel 2:28-32. The Holy Spirit was first "poured out" on the day of Pentecost in Acts 2 (hence the name Pentecostals), and this move of the Spirit is accelerating as the Lord's return fast approaches.

AN EXPERIENTIAL PERSPECTIVE

Perhaps hearing that a Spirit-led, worldwide end-times revival has been going on for more than a century excites you. But you're skeptical because your understanding of the baptism in the Holy Spirit is very different from what I have discussed so far. As I mentioned earlier, I am a third-generation Pentecostal.

Both my maternal and paternal grandparents accepted Jesus as their Savior and underwent noticeable transformations in their lives — including the ability to speak in a language they had never learned.

From my earliest recollections, there were "tongues-talkers" surrounding my life. During times of prayer, I would often hear my relatives and Christian friends quietly speaking in an unknown language. I would go to church and there would regularly be public messages in tongues followed by an interpretation. And none of this seemed odd. I was so blessed to grow up in that environment because I learned at a very early age that this blessing from God, when it is understood and practiced properly, is a valuable asset to the Christian life. To me it was such a natural part of being a follower of Jesus that I wouldn't have felt complete without it. I'm sure it was very much what it would have been like to be a first century believer. (I'll share more on that in the next chapter.)

To understand the "power boost" Jesus talked about in Acts 1:8 when discussing the baptism in the Holy Spirit, I would ask you to think in terms of an engine in a vehicle. There have been certain models over the years that got better mileage with a six-cylinder engine under the hood than the exact same vehicle equipped with just a four-cylinder engine. Why would that be? Because the vehicle was just heavy enough that it needed the larger motor to operate with optimum efficiency. The smaller engine had a task that was just too large to be handled without excessive effort.

In a similar example, in our large farmhouse in the northern Minnesota countryside, the previous owner had a furnace installed that was simply too small to cope with the occasional 30 below zero winter nights. That furnace would be running virtually all night, burning far more fuel than would have been required with a larger furnace. The task was just too large for the smaller furnace to handle without excessive effort.

In the same way, the average Christian who is committed to serving God, but has not yet received the baptism in the Holy Spirit with the evidence of speaking in tongues, generally finds it more challenging to achieve success in personal holiness and effective witnessing. Those who *are* Spirit-filled are equipped with extra supernatural power to accomplish these same goals with more efficiency and less difficulty. They're still far from perfect, but they do have an ever-present ally in their daily quest to live victoriously for the Lord.

CONCLUDING THOUGHT

It is my hope that I have succeeded in this chapter in establishing that there clearly is additional power for service that comes from the baptism in the Holy Spirit with the evidence of speaking in tongues. But why would that be? Why is there such a difference between the effectiveness of praying with our own understanding, and praying in a language we do not know?

We have to keep in mind that the greatest battle we have as Kingdom warriors is in the spirit realm. Ephesians 6:10-12 says:

> Finally, be strong in the Lord and in his mighty power. Put on the full armor of God so that you can take your stand against the devil's schemes. For our struggle is not against flesh and blood, but against the rulers, against the authorities, against the powers of this dark world and against the spiritual forces of evil in the heavenly realms.

Verse 18 goes on to say, "pray in the Spirit on all occasions." So when we pray in tongues we are engaging with the Holy Spirit directly in the spirit-realm battle.

Think of it as if He is a spy. The Holy Spirit is able to continually be in the enemy camp where the powers of darkness are always preparing new battle plans. When we are petitioning God using our own words and intellect, we can only pray within the limits of what we know. But when we pray in an unknown tongue, the Spirit is praying through us — way beyond our own knowledge of any situation — and in direct conformity with the will of God. That is why the baptism in the Holy Spirit is so powerful.

I know it can be kind of confusing, because praying in tongues is essentially God talking to God. Of course, it wouldn't be the first time this happened. God the Son, Jesus, prayed to God the Father regularly. So God the Holy Spirit praying to God the Father is not uncharacteristic.

I don't believe the triune nature of God could ever be fully understood by our finite minds. But one thing I do know is that God regularly chooses to accomplish His will through His people. Otherwise, why would we have to pray at all — in any language? After all, God knows all of our needs before we even open our mouths. We must understand that it is God's pleasure to use us, His willing vessels, to fulfill His purposes and plans. So when the Holy Spirit chooses to pray to God through us, we can consider ourselves to be blessed indeed!

13 – THE HOLY SPIRIT: OUR CLOSEST FRIEND

The only initial evidence we find in the Bible for the baptism in the Holy Spirit is speaking in an unknown language. This has great symbolic significance! Because if the Spirit controls the tongue to the point that we can speak a language we have never learned, then He has clearly been put in charge of a submitted life.

I would hope by now that it is clear the baptism in the Holy Spirit with the evidence of speaking in tongues is a real phenomenon that has been experienced not just by me, but by hundreds of millions. I sometimes wonder just how many Pentecostal believers there would have to be around the world before this doctrine would finally be accepted by all Christians as indisputable reality and truth from God.

But I know that there are millions of people throughout history who have witnessed supernatural experiences that came from a very dark spiritual source as well. In fact, over the years, there have actually been those who call themselves Christians who have claimed that speaking in tongues is a manifestation of the devil. So what can we count on as being the actual truth on this subject?

Well, as always, anything we believe about anything is only opinion unless it is based on the Word of God. So let's explore together what the Bible says about the wonderful, albeit controversial, doctrine of the baptism in the Holy Spirit.

It would be hard to discuss the issue without addressing it in terms of common questions related to the doctrine, as well as the common misconceptions. Now please remember, even though I am not a Bible scholar extraordinaire I have "witnessed the car crash." So as I just mentioned in the last chapter I can look at the topic with experiential, as well as biblical, knowledge. Nonetheless, with a doctrine that is so widely disputed in the Church I will be using a heavy dose of Bible passages to make sure that reason and truth overcome any preconceived ideas that might be incorrect.

FILLED TO OVERFLOWING

One question that is often asked: *Is the Spirit filling received during the baptism in the Holy Spirit different from the filling received at salvation?* The short answer is, "yes." In Romans 8:9-11, Paul writes:

> You, however, are controlled not by the sinful nature but by the Spirit, if the Spirit of God lives in you. And if anyone does not have the Spirit of Christ, he does not belong to Christ. But if Christ is in you, your body is dead because of sin, yet your spirit is alive because of righteousness. And if the Spirit of him who raised Jesus from the dead is living in you, he who raised Christ from the dead will also give life to your mortal bodies through the Spirit, who lives in you.

So the Holy Spirit clearly dwells in us when we become Christians. But He also manifests Himself in ways beyond salvation, something Pentecostals generally refer to as an "overflowing" of the Holy Spirit.

In the book of Acts, Luke (whom archeology has proven to be a very accurate historian) records many of the important events surrounding the first century church following the ascension of Jesus into heaven. In Acts 8:14-17, Luke writes:

> When the apostles in Jerusalem heard that Samaria had accepted the word of God, they sent Peter and John to them. When they arrived, they prayed for them that they might receive the Holy Spirit, because the Holy Spirit had not yet come upon any of them; they had simply been baptized into the name of the Lord Jesus. Then Peter and John placed their hands on them, and they received the Holy Spirit.

A later account in Acts 19:1-2,6 says:

> While Apollos was at Corinth, Paul took the road through the interior and arrived at Ephesus. There he found some disciples and asked them, "Did you receive the Holy Spirit when you believed?" They answered, "No, we have not even heard that there is a Holy Spirit."...When Paul placed his hands on them, the Holy Spirit came on them, and they spoke in tongues and prophesied.

In both of these instances, the people involved had undeniably already become believers in Jesus, but had not yet "received the Holy Spirit." So if we take what the Scriptures say at face value here, without any preconceived ideas, it is clear that the baptism in the Holy Spirit with the evidence of speaking in tongues is unquestionably different from the indwelling of the Spirit received at salvation.

In the June 13, 2010 edition of the Pentecostal Evangel magazine, Alton Garrison — who at the time was the assistant superintendent of the Assemblies of God — wrote:

> "Before you are saved, the Holy Spirit convicts you of sin and draws you to Jesus. That's salvation. The Holy Spirit resides in you after you become a Christian.

However, there is an additional and distinct ministry of the Holy Spirit called the baptism in the Holy Spirit. This provides believers with an empowering to witness and to live lives pleasing to God."

I mentioned in chapter 11 of this book that one of the reasons I completely avoid alcohol consumption is because it lowers inhibitions, making it easier to give in to sin. Conversely, if the baptism in the Holy Spirit enhances our ability to live more Christlike lives, why wouldn't we want to completely embrace it? As Garrison added in the same article:

"Out of this Baptism process, when our spirit is full, we are empowered beyond our abilities as our spirit overflows with His Holy Spirit. Human timidity is gone, replaced with boldness to share the gospel. Lethargic spiritual commitment is energized with an excitement for God and a deep devotion to serve Him. Love for Christ becomes active and foremost, bringing a desire for holiness, with a longing to read His word and win the lost. In other words, as a result of the Baptism we are supercharged with the mind and the heart of Jesus and enabled to do His work more effectively. That's the purpose of the Spirit-filled life."

INDISPUTABLE EVIDENCE

A second important question that is often asked: *Can a person be considered baptized in the Holy Spirit if they have never spoken in tongues?* To answer this question, I would remind you of what those Bible college students in Topeka, Kansas found in 1900-1901. In their Christmas break assignment, after much investigation and study, they concluded that in the Bible the initial evidence for the baptism in the Holy Spirit was consistently speaking in tongues — a manifestation they themselves sought and experienced shortly thereafter.

Among the Scriptures that supported their findings was Acts 2:4: "All of them were filled with the Holy Spirit and began to speak in other tongues as the Spirit enabled them." This was an outpouring of the Holy Spirit that specifically affected the Jews. In Acts 8:18-19 the Spirit was poured out on the Samaritans (who were part Jew and part Gentile): "When Simon saw that the Spirit was given at the laying on of the apostles' hands, he offered them money and said, 'Give me also this ability so that everyone on whom I lay my hands may receive the Holy Spirit.'" And in Acts 19:1-6, a passage that we looked at a few moments ago, the Spirit was poured out on the Gentiles at Ephesus.

In each case mentioned here except one, the initial evidence of the baptism in the Holy Spirit was speaking in tongues. In the other, there was something very spectacular and obvious happening that prompted Simon to offer money for the gift. Since this is not explained any further, there is no reason to believe the physical evidence was any different; it is really the only logical assumption.

Perhaps the clearest scriptural example of the inseparable connection between the baptism in the Holy Spirit and speaking in an unknown language can be found in Acts 10:44-46, the first time the manifestation is poured out on the Gentiles:

> While Peter was still speaking these words, the Holy Spirit came on all who heard the message. The circumcised believers who had come with Peter were astonished that the gift of the Holy Spirit had been poured out even on the Gentiles. For they heard them speaking in tongues and praising God.

It can't get any clearer than that. The circumcised believers, the Jews, knew that the Gentiles had received the gift of the Holy Spirit for one reason — they heard them speaking in tongues while they were praising God.

In a modern-day testimonial to the important understanding of speaking in tongues as the initial evidence of the baptism in the Holy Spirit, Thomas Trask, who was the general superintendent of the Assemblies of God from 1993 to 2007, shared an internet message with pastors. In his waning days as the top leader of the denomination, Pastor Trask spoke of a woman who had been at the altar in one of his previous churches. She told Trask that she believed she had received the baptism in the Holy Spirit that night, but had not spoken in tongues.

Now unquestionably, God can meet us in very special ways and His presence can be very real without the Baptism. So Trask did not minimize what she experienced, but He didn't affirm what she believed either. He merely encouraged her to keep seeking the baptism with the accompanying evidence of speaking in tongues. She later did receive that manifestation and began the wonderful adventure of the Spirit-filled life. Had Trask not encouraged her to continue seeking, she may have never experienced this powerful added blessing that God had for her.

Why do I, and hundreds of millions of other Christians, believe speaking in tongues is so important? James 3 is perhaps the consummate chapter relating to the tongue — how important it is to speak appropriately, and how difficult that can be. In verse 8 James writes that "no man can tame the tongue." That's why I believe the only initial evidence we find in the Bible for the baptism in the Holy Spirit is speaking in an unknown language. This has great symbolic significance! Because if the Spirit controls the tongue to the point that we can speak a language we have never learned, then He has clearly been put in charge of a submitted life.

It's just like a bit in the mouth of a horse in verse 3, or the rudder on a ship in verse 4. Those small pieces can control the direction of the much larger whole. When the Holy Spirit is in control of the tongue, He has also been put into a position to control the direction of the whole person.

I think it's important to mention that I have heard a believer or two in church quietly speaking in tongues who, despite their commitment to God, were not living a very godly life at the time. For a long period that puzzled me because, as Alton Garrison wrote, I knew that the baptism in the Holy Spirit provided believers with an empowering to live lives pleasing to God.

Then one day it occurred to me that God knows the end from the beginning. So I came to the realization that when these people received His Holy Spirit baptism with the evidence of speaking in tongues despite their rough edges, it was because God knew that their commitment to Him would eventually translate to growing righteousness in their lives.

Sure enough, I ran into one of these individuals several years later and he had indeed made remarkable strides in his sanctification. He had gone from occasional drunkenness and even jail time, to a marriage with a godly wife and two children. He was also serving on the board at his church. Only God could have seen that coming so many years earlier.

NO CHILD OF GOD LEFT BEHIND

The third common question I'm going to address will be: *Is the baptism in the Holy Spirit available to all believers?* Again, the answer is an unambiguous, "yes."

To make the point, I will highlight a few verses here that we have already looked at — Acts 2:4, Acts 10:44, and Acts 19:6. If you are able to take the time to reread these passages, you will see that in each case *all* people who were present were filled with the Holy Spirit and spoke in tongues. In other words, the blessing was not selective.

In anticipation of the argument some might have that this was only true for first century believers, I have some modern day examples to share as well. A close relative of mine experienced the baptism in the Holy Spirit with the evidence of speaking in tongues for the first time at a conference which featured a group that prayed regularly for people to receive this special manifestation. To their knowledge, under their ministry virtually every person who sincerely sought the baptism was filled — including my relative. This was typical of what we saw in the book of Acts. My personal experience was much the same. I spoke in tongues for the first time, albeit to a very minimal degree, at a youth retreat where several other young people also received the baptism.

In order to claim that the baptism in the Holy Spirit with the evidence of speaking in tongues is *not* available to all Christians, you would have to believe that in these real-world instances God carefully brought together just those people who were intended to receive and no one else. While God certainly *could* have done this, it stretches credibility to believe He actually *would* have done this. No, it makes much more sense to believe that this amazing blessing from God is a gift He wants to bestow upon *all* of His children to aid them in their walk with Christ. That was certainly the experience of the first century believers.

PRIVATE AND PERSONAL, OR PUBLIC AND PROPHETIC

This leads to another closely-associated question that is commonly asked when discussing the baptism in the Holy Spirit: *Is there a difference between tongues as a private, personal prayer language, and tongues in a public assembly?* This is an important question to answer because it has been the subject of great confusion among believers.

One time several years ago I was discussing the baptism in the Holy Spirit with a co-worker who was resistant to the doctrine. He finally conceded that he believed tongues could be a valid manifestation of the Holy Spirit, but that he would only recognize it as legitimate if there was an immediate interpretation.

This is not an unusual belief among Christians. So let's take a comprehensive look at what the Bible has to say to bring some clarity to the issue.

While tongues as a personal prayer language is available to all believers, tongues in a public assembly — such as a church service — is a selective prophetic gifting bestowed by the Holy Spirit. Paul wrote the book of 1 Corinthians to address some incorrect practices and beliefs that had invaded the church he had founded in Corinth, Greece, including those surrounding public worship. Chapter 12 is about the spiritual gifts given by the Holy Spirit to believers "for the common good" in an assembly. Among them, as written in verse 10: "...to another different kinds of tongues, and to still another the interpretation of tongues."

Additionally, in verses 27-31 Paul touches on the ministry gifts along with spiritual gifts, again mentioning tongues and interpretations. In the New American Standard version of the Bible, Paul asks the questions in verse 30: "All do not speak with tongues, do they? All do not interpret, do they?" Paul then goes on to call these, along with a list of other prophetic gifts, the "greater gifts" and says we should earnestly seek them.

Now it has to be pointed out that if there is no difference between the speaking in tongues mentioned in the book of Acts, and the gift of tongues as written about in the book of 1 Corinthians, then the Bible contains a complete contradiction. As we have already seen, *all* believers present in the book of Acts who had not yet received the baptism in the Holy Spirit were routinely prayed for. And with regularity, *all* who were present began to speak in tongues. Yet here in 1 Corinthians, we are told that the gift of tongues is *selectively* bestowed by the Holy Spirit; not all receive it. We know that the Bible never contradicts itself when the full context is understood. So what is the difference between these two otherwise similar manifestations?

Some clarification can be found in 1 Corinthians 14. Paul alternately writes of tongues as a private, personal prayer language, and tongues as a prophetic gifting. In verses 1-3:

> Follow the way of love and eagerly desire spiritual gifts, especially the gift of prophecy. For anyone who speaks in a tongue does not speak to men but to God. Indeed, no one understands him; he utters mysteries with his spirit. But everyone who prophesies speaks to men for their strengthening, encouragement and comfort.

What Paul is saying here is that the personal prayer language (which is first discussed in Acts) is a private conversation between the Christian and God. But even better is the greater *prophetic* gifting of tongues which edifies others as well. As Paul says in verse 4: "He who speaks in a tongue edifies himself, but he who prophesies edifies the church." And while the personal prayer language does not require an interpretation because it is a conversation directly with God, verses 13-17 tell us that a prophetic message in tongues in an assembly *is* to be followed by an interpretation. Otherwise the message is meaningless to the congregation.

It should also be pointed out that in verse 5 where it says, "I would like every one of you to speak in tongues, but I would rather have you prophesy," Paul is not saying tongues are not important. He is just giving teaching to the Corinthian church on the proper use of tongues in an assembly. The same can be said for verses 18 and 19:

> I thank God that I speak in tongues more than all of you [personal prayer language]. But in the church I would rather speak five intelligible words to instruct others than ten thousand words in a tongue [prophetic gifting].

Again, Paul is conveying here that a message in tongues in an assembly is meaningless unless it is followed by an interpretation.

THE OLD AND NEW NORMAL

The teaching throughout 1 Corinthians chapters 12 and 14 should make it clear that speaking in tongues was the norm among first century believers. Paul is obviously writing with the assumption that all of the readers are acquainted with this manifestation. So he doesn't give a remedial explanation or defend the use of tongues, he merely gives instruction on how the prophetic gift should be properly used in an assembly.

Just as an aside, have you ever wondered why 1 Corinthians 13, "the love chapter," is nestled right in the middle of all this doctrinal teaching on spiritual gifts? It seems like peculiar positioning. But like a world-class chess player, the Holy Spirit never wastes a move. I believe it was placed there because if we speak in tongues and operate in the gifts of the Spirit, but do not demonstrate a consistent life of selfless, Christlike love, then our witness essentially becomes ineffective and meaningless.

That is also why speaking in tongues has to be just the starting point of a Spirit-filled life. Indeed, we should continue to seek refillings regularly so our spiritual gas tanks don't go empty. And we should also regularly ask God for the "greater" spiritual gifts to be manifest in our lives, and that the fruit of the Spirit as described in Galatians 5:22-23 would be increasingly evident in and through us.

RECEIVING IS BELIEVING

Perhaps you've been feeling the nudge of the Holy Spirit as you've been reading and want to personally experience His baptism — but you don't know where to start. There is really no one specific way to go about it. As I've mentioned in some of the previous examples, many people speak in tongues for the first time while being prayed for by others. Seek out a Pentecostal church, or go to a seminar, revival, or conference in which the focus is Spirit baptism and ask to be prayed for.

This of course is a biblical approach, matching the experiences of the first century believers we read about in the book of Acts.

Others will testify to receiving the baptism in the Holy Spirit while alone, maybe as they prayed in bed or even while driving a car. One lady who spoke in tongues for the first time while on the highway said she almost drove off the road because the tears of joy made it hard for her to see! She said she just prayed, "God, I'm tired of my ineffective faith. I want all that you would have for me." And the Lord responded by filling her on the spot.

That is the key — seeking after all God has for you. Ask Him to fill to you to overflowing with His Holy Spirit and then be expecting a positive answer to this prayer. As Jesus said in Luke 11:11-13:

> Which of you fathers, if your son asks for a fish, will give him a snake instead? Or if he asks for an egg, will give him a scorpion? If you then, though you are evil, know how to give good gifts to your children, how much more will your Father in heaven give the Holy Spirit to those who ask Him!

When you are praying for this precious gift, if even a syllable or two comes to mind go ahead and speak it. This is often the way the Spirit baptism begins. And then continue to pray for more; not necessarily for more of a language, but more of God. A number of people have testified to me that it took months, and even years, for them to receive the baptism in the Holy Spirit. What finally brought the breakthrough was when they stopped seeking after the unknown tongue, and instead just sought after more of God. Then the release came and they experienced the joy of this most intimate relationship with Him.

When you do receive and begin speaking in a language you have never learned, don't doubt it. Satan does not like what just happened and he will do whatever he can to snatch this blessing from you. He'll seek to make you doubt what you have experienced, and will likely bring willing vessels into your life to try to convince you that it is not an actual manifestation from God. At these times, seek your heart; you will know the real source of this amazing gift!

I have one final admonition. After you have received, continue to speak in your prayer language on a regular basis. The baptism in the Holy Spirit is not meant to be a one-time event. It is meant to be a lifestyle that will continue to help you in your personal spiritual growth, and in your ability to serve the Lord with more effectiveness and power.

CONCLUDING THOUGHT

As I bring this chapter to a close I'd like to talk deeply from the heart, perhaps with more conviction that I have ever used in my books thus far. I understand any skepticism you might have about the interpretation of this doctrine as I have presented it; unless you grew up in a Pentecostal church you likely have not heard it taught this way.

So why did I decide to include such a controversial teaching in this book, despite the fact that so many will continue to disagree with me? As we have seen, the baptism in the Holy Spirit with the evidence of speaking in tongues is discussed at length in Scripture so it's not some fringe doctrine. It was an integral part of the life of first century believers and I believe it is just as important for us to embrace it today.

When the Holy Spirit fell on the believers gathered in Acts 2 and they spoke in tongues, Peter himself said in verse 17 that this was fulfillment of the prophecy found in Joel 2:28-32: "In the last days, God says, I will pour out my Spirit on all people." And this prophecy was expanded into an end times admonition in Jude 1:20-21: "But you, dear friends, build yourselves up in your most holy faith and pray in the Holy Spirit. Keep yourselves in God's love as you wait for the mercy of our Lord Jesus Christ to bring you to eternal life."

There is nowhere is Scripture telling us that the last days have come to an end. And now, for more than one hundred years, we have seen modern historical and experiential evidence that this manifestation of the Spirit is continuing. As I mentioned earlier, since the Azusa Street Revival began in 1906, the modern Pentecostal movement has grown from a handful of believers to more than 600 million. That's the second largest group of professed Christians in the world behind only Catholicism, which has existed for many more centuries!

So this is why I felt a discussion on the doctrine of the baptism in the Holy Spirit was vital in a book focused on being victorious as Christians. The power to effectively reach souls for Christ isn't just for the very gifted evangelists like Charles Spurgeon, D.L. Moody, or Billy Graham. It is also available to each of us as "everyday" Kingdom warriors.

I trust you feel as I do. I want all of the supernatural power that is available to reach my unsaved friends and loved ones for Christ. Please don't let any abuses practiced in ignorance, or the silly displays of some in the name of Spirit baptism, keep you from seeking this powerful blessing from God. That is exactly what Satan would want — for you to find reasons to doubt the validity of this amazing gift. My dear brothers and sisters in Christ, I encourage you to join me in chasing after God so that the power of the Holy Spirit in each one of us can break through strongholds to touch lives for His Kingdom. Eternal life or death is in the balance!

14–DEPLOYED FOR BATTLE

I believe with all my heart that these "radical" steps of self-less dedication, when consistently lived out in the lives of Christ followers, will make a real difference for eternity as people are irresistibly drawn to Jesus through our example.

In recent years, wildfires in California have become very newsworthy. As housing and business development continues to move into additional areas of existing forests and other vegetative growth, these fires have begun to damage more property and claim more lives. The financial costs often go into the hundreds of millions, while the tragic fatal human cost has at times reached into the dozens.

Sometimes, authorities are able to determine what started these blazes. Sparks from a hammer, flames from a backyard barbecue, a torch cutting metal, a downed power line, a carelessly tossed cigarette butt, a hot vehicle tailpipe, and lightning — these are just a few of the known causes of several massive wildfires that have burned through the California countryside and mountains in recent years.

Although these fires began in varied ways, one thing was constant. Each of these destructive blazes started with a tiny flame, sometimes even just a spark. And as we are now in the final chapter, that is what I am praying will happen with this book — but obviously in a completely positive way.

I hate to admit it, I have only a mustard seed of faith that my message will create much of a "blaze." Even if *Kingdom Warriors* has sales beyond my wildest dreams, it would still only reach a tiny percentage of the people in the nation. And for those who do buy and read the book, a smaller percentage still are going to take it to heart and actually follow through on my concerns and recommendations. So it is my prayer that those of you who *are* truly passionate about living a life of radical devotion to God will have an amazing impact for the Kingdom, like tiny sparks that grow into massive wildfires.

THE PAST

Let's face it, it's going to take something truly radical to bring about a positive change. The morality in our country has been headed in a downward trajectory ever since 1962 when prayer and Bible reading were no longer allowed in our public schools thanks to decisions by the U.S. Supreme Court. This marked the first time in its nearly 200-year history that the government of the United States said, in effect, "no" to the living God. And the results are becoming increasingly palpable.

Maybe you've heard about the studies which looked at the biggest problems reported by teachers in public school classrooms during the twentieth century. In the 1940's when my mom and dad were in high school, the most prominent discipline issues included chewing gum, making noise in class, and not putting trash paper in wastebaskets. By the 1980's, the first generation that was censored from biblical moral guidance in the public schools was growing up. And their discipline problems in high school reflected a startling change. The biggest issues reported by teachers had become rape, robbery, assault, and suicide just to name a few. And as we've moved into the twenty-first century, homicidal violence with multiple fatalities has become an all too common occurrence in our schools.

Academic achievement among the nation's students has also taken a notable nosedive since 1962. According to

Wallbuilders, a ministry that documents the Christian heritage of our nation, as early as 2004 there had been a sharp decline in SAT scores which measure the college readiness of high school seniors. In international testing, these same students had moved to last, near last, or in the bottom half in math and science. And America ranked 65th out of 200 countries in terms of literacy. Prior to 1962, literacy in the U.S. was number one in the world.

It's interesting to note too that as recently as the 2004 election when President George W. Bush won a second term in the White House, about one-third of the voters in exit polls said moral issues reflecting biblical values were the number one influence on how they cast their ballots. I was so proud of the people of our nation at that time. What a testimony to the world of our Judeo-Christian values!

But those same kids who grew up starting in the 1960's without a Christian-based moral compass in the public schools now make up the majority of voters and leaders of our nation. And we are seeing the results of that today as morality is tanking fast. Let's take a look at some of what has happened in our culture in just the last decade or two, much of which I have already discussed in detail in previous chapters.

Gambling has gone from a largely spurned practice limited in its access, to a readily-available, socially-acceptable activity. The number of casinos across the country has grown to the point where the vast majority of Americans now have one within a couple-hundred miles of where they live. So it no longer requires a commitment of a day or more, and perhaps several hundred dollars, just to get to a casino in order to participate in gambling activity.

Even more accessible is online wagering, which has received greater sanction from the government as well. This includes a 2018 U.S. Supreme Court ruling that legalized betting on sports nationwide. Within a year, the legislatures in no less than eight states had already voted to make the practice legal.

The promise of increased tax revenue is generally the largest driving factor in decisions to make gambling legal and more available — but at what cost? As we saw in chapter 10 of this book, the result of moves such as these has been a tragic rise in divorce, suicide, and crime rates related to gambling.

Alcohol consumption is a major factor in most fatal traffic crashes, and is involved in the vast majority of serious crimes including child and spousal abuse, sexual assaults, and homicides. Yet inexplicably, it continues to gain acceptability in the culture. One example includes the extra freedom given to the brewers of "craft beers" to produce their product. Deregulation and lower excise taxes have coupled to create a boom in the craft beer industry in the last few decades.

In an article entitled "Beer Boom" in the Winter 2019 edition of *Thinking Minnesota* magazine published by the Center of the American Experiment, John Phelan wrote, "One group estimated that 78.5 percent of drinking-aged adults in America live within 10 miles of a brewery." Phelan also pointed to the dramatic growth of the industry in my home state of Minnesota. He wrote, "The pace of this beer change has been staggering. In 2007, there were fewer than 10 breweries and brewpubs statewide. A decade later, the total number has reached over 170 (an increase of 1,600 percent)."

Another common change related to alcoholic beverages in recent years is the extended hours of legal consumption approved by local and state governments. Each of these things is being praised for adding jobs, and as with gambling, increasing governmental income from taxes. But again, at what cost to individuals, families, and society as a whole?

Here's a rather mind-numbing statistic: Among my fellow residents in Minnesota, one in seven drivers on the road has at least one DWI on their record! And I would be sure that other states have a similar rate. Is this going to get better now that alcohol is finding more acceptance and accessibility? I found it interesting that in the same week Minnesota legalized liquor sales on Sundays for the first time, a woman was killed by a drunk driver in a hit-and-run crash in Minneapolis. And across the country during a Mardi Gras celebration in New Orleans, police said a "highly-intoxicated" man was responsible for driving into a crowd, injuring 29 people.

Marijuana is also gaining increased acceptance. Although I haven't mentioned the drug in previous chapters, I feel it deserves a mention before I conclude this book. Because as of this writing, the recreational use of marijuana is being legalized in state after state.

When I was in high school in the 1970's we used to call those who regularly smoked pot "burn-outs" because their inability to learn and function responsibly was often very obvious. I doubt the effects of marijuana use on the body and mind has changed for the better in the last few decades. In fact, thanks to changes in the way the plant is produced, recent studies have indicated that the marijuana sold at legal dispensaries today is actually five times higher in THC — the substance that causes the brain-damaging "high" — than the pot used when I was in high school.

In the fall of 2019, the fast-forward acceptance of recreational marijuana use in the culture prompted a concerned U.S. Surgeon General Jerome Adams to issue an advisory. He wrote: "Recent increases in access to marijuana and in its potency, along with misperceptions of safety of marijuana endanger our most precious resource, our nation's youth." In addition, Adams wrote that "no amount of marijuana use during pregnancy or adolescence is known to be safe."

And yet, once again, the ability to tax and regulate are given as prime reasons to legalize the drug. But, dare I say it one more time, at what cost? In states that have already legalized marijuana for recreational use, there has been a notable increase in related traffic fatalities, poison control calls, and arrests of youth, as well as a growing black market for pot sales.

Finally, and most importantly, **marriage** has gone from its understood place as a critical foundation of society, to an optional place in which to have self-serving needs met for as long as a couple wants to stay together. And we are seeing a steady cultural decline as a result. Statistics regularly confirm that children who come from divorced or never-married homes are more likely to live in poverty, fail in school and employment, abuse drugs, and have physical and mental health issues.

And the very definition of marriage has been changed nationwide to allow for the legal union of same-sex couples. This comes despite the fact that in 1996, not that long ago, Congress overwhelmingly passed the Defense of Marriage Act with bipartisan support. It affirmed that the only marriages recognized by the federal government as legal were those that fit the biblical definition – one man with one woman.

THE PRESENT

There is historical precedent for a belief that this moral free fall will continue in the United States. Nations that have gone through extended periods of relative peace, military dominance, and affluence such as we have experienced over the last several decades have regularly gone from a collective mindset of mere survival, to a more inward, narcissistic approach to life. When people lose sight of the need for God's protection and provision it is easy to take on an arrogant, humanistic perspective, thinking that we can solve all problems with our own strength, wisdom, and resources.

This is why Jesus said to His disciples in Matthew 19:23, "I tell you the truth, it is hard for a rich man to enter the kingdom of heaven." When we have measure of wealth it is so easy to become self-reliant, forgetting about or overlooking our need for God and His salvation. The concerns for the day revolve largely around what to eat, rather than if we will eat; and what to spend our money on, rather than if we will have any money to spend.

Perhaps the most glaring example of the drift toward narcissistic humanism would be the Roman Empire of Jesus' time. As the Romans gained more and more military conquests, and their enemies became essentially powerless to fight against them, the citizens of Rome grew more and more consumed with fulfilling their own lusts and pleasures. This included increasingly violent and sexually immoral entertainment and behavior. The result was a country that was not defeated by an outside enemy, but in essence, was destroyed from within.

I fear the citizens of the United States are on the same path. There is arguably no existential threat to our nation from without; no country or terrorist group would have any realistic ability to conquer us. And our collective wealth is beyond what any nation has ever experienced in human history. So we have descended largely into a country that is ignorantly consumed with destroying itself from within, mirroring the fall of the Roman empire of long ago.

The art and literature of that time indicated that Rome had become self-consumed and morally bankrupt before losing its world dominance, including depictions of graphic violence and sexual depravity — not unlike what we are already seeing in America today. Much of what is currently considered art or entertainment in the U.S., including even some of what can be seen on prime-time television, is utterly vulgar and disgusting. The biblical moral compass is clearly gone.

THE FUTURE

Although I have already touched on some of our country's moral decay in recent years, I believe we are only seeing the tip of the iceberg. While I'm no prophet, I believe there are some things that are predictable based on the current trajectory of things in our culture.

I fully expect that restrictions on virtually all forms of gambling will continue to fall as federal, state, and local governments continue to look for new ways to pay for ever-expanding social programs in our increasingly entitlement-minded society. And step-by-step, the various forms of online wagering will become universally legal. These moves would lead to an unprecedented epidemic of gambling addiction among all ages as wagering could be legally done virtually anywhere at any time. The result would be even more gambling-related divorces, suicides, and crime rates.

I believe that restrictions on alcohol consumption that have literally been in place for centuries will continue to be repealed by governmental entities. Any remaining state and local laws prohibiting alcohol sales on Sundays or at certain other times will be removed, and it's quite possible that the federal government will once again allow states to lower the legal drinking age to 18 from the current 21. The reasoning will be that 18-year-olds can fight and die in wars, so why shouldn't they be allowed to drink? This would result in an epidemic of alcoholism among younger and younger individuals and the predictable outcome of even more alcohol-related deaths and assaults on college campuses, broken homes, traffic fatalities, and crime.

I'm of the belief that not only will the recreational use of marijuana be legalized eventually in all 50 states, but other types of drugs will also be made legal. The argument will be that legalized marijuana has been a financial boon for states because its sale can now be taxed, and less law enforcement resources are needed to arrest and incarcerate violators, so why not make other drugs legal for the same reasons? This will provide a similar opportunity to regulate their use.

I even heard one politician say he trusts adults to make the right decisions in regards to their drug use. Oddly, this was at the same time literally tens of thousands of people were dying every year as a result of their uncontrolled addiction to opioids. Overdose deaths from other drugs would certainly become epidemic as well if they are made legal.

I have very little doubt that God's design for marriage, one man with one woman for life, will continue to come under attack. It will become basically "anything goes" as to who can marry who. It will be all about "love." It won't matter what gender they are, or how close of relatives they are (yes, even incest), or how old they are (yes, even children) — the only consideration will be that they "love" one another.

Numbers won't matter either. I expect that polygamy will eventually become legal because it will be considered discriminatory and frivolous to prevent numerous people from consensually sharing their love together. In fact, in July of 2020 the city council in Somerville, Massachusetts voted to legally recognize "polyamory." This enabled groups of three or more people to register with the city and obtain the same rights as married couples. And there was also a movement afoot in the Utah Legislature to make polygamy an "infraction" rather than a felony, which would remove the threat of jail time for violators.

Of course, this would only apply if people make marriage a consideration at all. Sexual expression will likely be looked at as acceptable in any form, just as long as each party involved is consenting. This relational and sexual free-for-all would be the ultimate form of narcissism, and the culture would begin an accelerated collapse as the foundational family design established by God Himself would crumble.

Should this last prediction come to pass, I believe it would contribute to the fulfillment of a prophecy found in 2 Timothy 3:1-4:

But mark this: There will be terrible times in the last days. People will be lovers of themselves, lovers of money, boastful, proud, abusive, disobedient to their parents, ungrateful, unholy, without love, unforgiving, slanderous, without self-control, brutal, not lovers of good, treacherous, rash, conceited, lovers of pleasure rather than lovers of God...

These behaviors are already becoming more and more evident today, and will get even worse if our culture continues on its current downward moral trajectory.

CONCLUDING THOUGHT

When I am working in my news director's job in radio, one of the fun things I do with the morning show host on two of our stations is make predictions on the air about what I believe will happen with our sports teams. Will they be better than last season? Will they make it to the playoffs? Will they win the championship? Even though I'd like to think I'm an expert, I am only right probably half the time. In other words, I only do just about as well as the next guy. That's because there are so many uncontrolled variables. The team could suffer multiple injuries, they could trade a key player, or players just don't live up to expectations.

The way I see it, when it comes to the predictions I have just made in this chapter there is really only one variable that will turn the tide. And that's if Christians en masse get very serious about their faith, living lives radically devoted to God. I have given my perspectives throughout this book on how to effectively accomplish that mission.

The words of Paul in 1 Thessalonians 5:23-24 serve both as a benediction and an exhortation:

May God himself, the God of peace, sanctify you through and through. May your whole spirit, soul and body be kept blameless at the coming of our Lord Jesus Christ.

There are certain popular sayings I have mentioned in this book with which I largely disagree — and I'd like to add just one more: "Preach the Gospel, and if necessary, use words." Sadly I feel this message is too often used as an excuse to remain silent when we really need to be courageously sharing our faith with people. But I do agree with the sentiment behind the statement — that our sanctified attitudes, actions, and activities should point so well to the God we represent that words almost aren't even necessary to reveal the source of the godly behavior people see in us.

I encourage you to wake up each morning with a prayer that God will bring people into your life that you can touch for the Kingdom. When those opportunities come, pray that God will give you the right words to say, and that His light will shine through you, reflecting a sanctified life that points to Jesus.

Sanctified attitudes exhibit a Christ-likeness toward people; loving them unconditionally and showing them unexpected respect and kindness. This would include those we know — our families, friends, and co-workers — and those we don't know such as the telemarketer, waiter or waitress, or customer service representative.

Sanctified actions exemplify Christ as well. People will be pleasantly overwhelmed by the fruit of the Spirit when they interact with us, experiencing the love, joy, peace, patience, kindness, goodness, faithfulness, gentleness, and self-control spoken of in Galatians 5:22-23.

And sanctified activities allow no concern for compromise. It will be clear through what we do — including how and where we spend our money and time, and what we consume into our bodies and minds — that we are choosing to lovingly commit our lives to a holy and righteous God who is unquestionably worthy of such honor.

I believe with all my heart that these "radical" steps of selfless dedication, when consistently lived out in the lives of Christ followers, will make a real difference for eternity as people are irresistibly drawn to Jesus through our example. This type of devotion to God will truly make us effective, victorious warriors for His Kingdom!

ENDNOTES

1   Randy Kennedy. *Kingdom Invaders: Postmodern Threats to Biblical Christianity* (Maitland, FL: Xulon Press, 2015)

2   Nabeel Qureshi. *Seeking Allah, Finding Jesus* (Grand Rapids, MI: Zondervan, 2014)

3   William Paul Young. *The Shack* (Los Angeles, CA: Windblown Media, 2007)

4   William Paul Young. *The Lies We Believe About God* (New York, NY: Atria Books, 2017)

5   L. Ron Hubbard. *Dianetics, the Modern Science of Mental Health* (Los Angeles, CA: Bridge Publications, Inc., 1950)

6   G.A. Prichard. *Willow Creek Seeker Services* (Chicago, IL: Baker, 1996) 264

7   Bob Showers. *Minnesota North Stars History and Memories with Lou Nanne* (Edina, MN: Beaver's Pond Press, 2007)

8   Jerry Bridges. *The Pursuit of Holiness* (Colorado Springs, CO: NavPress, 2006) 72

9   Janette Oke. *Love's Long Journey* (Bloomington, MN: Bethany House Publishers, 1982, 2003)

10 Brennan Manning. *The Ragamuffin Gospel* (Colorado Springs, CO: Multnomah Books, 1990)

11 A.W. Tozer. *The Pursuit of God* (Camp Hill, PA: Wing Spread Publishers, 1948,1982,1993,2006) 99

12 Rex M. Rogers. *Gambling: Don't Bet On It* (Grand Rapids, MI: Kregel Publications, 2005) 170

13 Rogers. *Gambling: Don't Bet On It*, 121

14 Rogers. *Gambling: Don't Bet On It*, 170

CPSIA information can be obtained
at www.ICGtesting.com
Printed in the USA
FSHW021902231020

9 781632 211569